Studies in Jungian Thought
JAMES HILLMAN, General Editor

A volume from the *Studies from the* C. G. *Jung Institute, Zurich*

Conscience

ESSAYS BY
Hans Zbinden   Eugen Böhler
R. J. Zwi Werblowsky   Hans Schär
Josef Rudin   Ernst Blum   C. G. Jung
Translated by R. F. C. Hull and Ruth Horine

EDITED BY
The Curatorium of the C. G. Jung Institute,
Zurich

Northwestern University Press
Evanston   1970

COPYRIGHT © 1970 BY NORTHWESTERN UNIVERSITY PRESS
LIBRARY OF CONGRESS CATALOG CARD NUMBER: 77–98465
SBN: 8101–0297–8
Composed in Janson and Melior types, printed, and bound by
Kingsport Press, Inc., Kingsport, Tennessee.

The original German-language edition of CONSCIENCE was published in 1958 by Rascher Verlag, Zurich and Stuttgart, under
the title *Das Gewissen, Studien aus dem C. G. Jung-Institut
Zürich, Vol. VII.*

"A Psychological View of Conscience," by C. G. Jung, originally appeared in the translation by R. F. C. Hull in *The Collected Works of C. G. Jung*, Volume X, copyright © 1964
by the Bollingen Foundation; published by the Bollingen
Foundation in the United States and by Routledge and Kegan
Paul Ltd. in England. It is reprinted here by permission of
the Bollingen Foundation, Routledge and Kegan Paul Ltd.,
and the heirs of Dr. Jung.

CONTENTS

PREFACE TO THE
AMERICAN EDITION

THIS BOOK brings together seven different perspectives upon the phenomenon of the human conscience. These chapters were originally presented as individual lectures under the auspices of the C. G. Jung Institute, Zurich, during the winter semester, 1957–58.

Conscience is yet another area of the psyche which psychology alone cannot encompass. To circumscribe conscience we must turn elsewhere: to the religions, the history of social culture, economic contexts, and also to therapeutic psychology. At least seven hands are necessary to shape our theme, and perhaps a dozen more would still not be sufficient, since conscience is essential to what we call "human."

The moral quality of human nature receives less attention in psychology today than it did when psychology was a handmaiden of philosophy and theology. The advent of scientific psychology, and its secularization, has tended to place the moral component of human nature at one remove, just as natural science has generally divorced itself from the moral preoccupations of the prescientific era. As long as the psyche is conceived as a natural concomitant to physiology or the result of social forces, conscience is only a biological or social derivative. But the moment we realize that the psyche is but another word for soul, then the problem of the morality of the human person—his sin, guilt, atonement, and the structure and contents of the conscience—assumes radical importance again.

This book by no means exhausts the theme, but it will serve its purpose if it provokes psychology to end its neglect of the moral nature of man and to remember that conscience is bound up with all man's actions whatever the sphere in which they are enacted. Unless we recognize this basic truth, we move without knowing it from the "age of anxiety" into the "age of psychopathy" or "moral insanity," which is best defined as a lacuna or absence of the moral sense. Anxiety at least reflects conscience. In its neurotic worry over right and wrong, it points to a moral sense. In psychopathy, concern is just not there; it is amoral. In an age of psychopathy, happenings matter only to our appetites, our ambitions, or our image, but they do not matter to our souls. Horrors may multiply, but we would not feel them, for we would then have lost the ability to be appalled. There would be no moral reaction. The computer has been declared inhuman because it does not fulfill the biological and social definitions of what is human. But it is also inhuman because it has no conscience; it is an efficiently cool psychopath. Yet we turn to it for "decision-making." This volume reminds us that decisions can have another guide, the individual conscience. The conscience of the individual might even be said to be the essence of his individuality. In the quantitative world of masses and powers, its still, small voice seems weak indeed. But there, in that weakness, individuality begins. On what else can human dignity be built if not on the sense of oneself as a moral being? These papers turn our attention in this direction, thereby leading us into the psychological heart of the contemporary predicament.

A WORD ON THE AUTHORS: Hans Zbinden, professor of cultural sociology at the University of Bern, is well known in Switzerland in the fields of social sciences and literature. His many publications include *Die Moralkrise des Abendlandes* (The Moral Crisis of the West), *Ohnmacht der Eliten* (The Impotence of the Elite), and *Mensch und Technik* (Man and Technology). Eugen Böhler, professor of national economics, finance, and statistics at the Federal Institute of Technology, Zurich, has for several decades contributed actively to Swiss current affairs as a theoretician and critic. He was a friend of

C. G. Jung and served as Curatorium member and as a Patron
of the C. G. Jung Institute. R. J. Z. Werblowsky, dean of the
faculty of humanities of the Hebrew University, Jerusalem, is
known mainly as a scholar in the history of religions; of his
writings, *Lucifer and Prometheus* and *Joseph Karo: Lawyer
and Mystic* have been published in English. The late Hans
Schär was professor of church history and the psychology of
religion at the University of Bern. His major work, *Erlösung-
vorstellungen und ihre psychologischen Aspekte,* appeared as
Volume 2 of the *Studien aus dem C. G. Jung-Institut Zürich,*
of which series this present book was Volume 7; his *Religion
and the Cure of Souls* was published in the Bollingen Series.
Josef Rudin has had long experience with the interrelations
of analytical psychology and Catholic theology. His teaching
activities extend from Switzerland to Germany and Austria,
where he is now professor of pastoral psychology at the University of Innsbruck. His work *Fanatismus* (Fanaticism) has
been translated into several languages, including English. Ernst
Blum is professor in the medical faculty at the University of
Bern. His work is in the fields of neurology, psychiatry, and
psychoanalysis. He is one of the senior Freudian psychiatrists
in Switzerland. C. G. Jung needs no introduction to the American reader. His essay in this volume may also be found in
Civilization in Transition, Volume 10 of his *Collected Works.*
We are grateful to the Bollingen Foundation and to Dr. Jung's
heirs for permission to reproduce his essay here in the context
for which it was originally written.

The translations were prepared by Mr. R. F. C. Hull and
Mrs. Ruth Horine. Mr. Hull is responsible alone for the essays
by R. J. Z. Werblowsky, E. Blum, and C. G. Jung. Mrs. Horine
translated the essay by E. Böhler. The remaining papers are the
result of collaboration between Mr. Hull and Mrs. Horine. Mr.
John Friesen also contributed to the translation of Dr. Schär's
essay. The late Mr. A. S. B. Glover collaborated on the scholarly apparatus. The index was prepared by Mrs. Horine and
Dr. Daveda Tenenbaum.

The original German edition of *Conscience* was edited by

the Curatorium of the C. G. Jung Institute, Zurich. The translations in this volume depart only now and again from the original, and where they do it is at the author's own wish to condense or revise. In some cases the translators have made their own renderings of quotations in the texts, but wherever possible the sources and texts cited have been presented in their standard English versions.

Zurich, 1969   JAMES HILLMAN

INTRODUCTION

In organizing a lecture series on "Conscience" apart from our regular training program for analysts, we wished to focus discussion on a particularly burning problem of general interest.

Because the subject is so complex, it was impossible to consider it from all the aspects of human and intellectual endeavor. We therefore found ourselves obliged to limit discussion to some of its more significant features. These were highlighted in the course of seven lectures delivered by different persons, each outstanding in his own specific scientific or scholarly field of activity.

The momentous importance which must be attributed to the problem of conscience in our day—more than at any previous time in history—was undoubtedly responsible for the great popularity which these lectures enjoyed. Their wide appeal induced us to publish them, in the order in which they were delivered, as the seventh volume of the series entitled *Studien aus dem C. G. Jung-Institut Zürich* with a view to making them accessible to a broader section of the public. We also wish to take this opportunity to express once more our appreciation and gratitude to all those who contributed to this publication.

THE CURATORIUM OF THE
C. G. JUNG INSTITUTE

Zurich
Spring, 1958

Conscience in Our Time

Hans Zbinden

Translated by Ruth Horine

THE FIRST CHAPTER in this timely volume has been entrusted not to a scientific psychologist nor to a moralist or theologian but to a critical observer of culture from the field of sociology. So if, in what follows, we ask about "Conscience in Our Time" we do so not in order to devote ourselves to philosophical or psychological investigations, nor yet to approach the problem from the standpoint of a given religious doctrine; rather we are impelled by a question as elementary as it is inescapable: What is the position of conscience today? What is its effectiveness —or impotence—in modern society?

Thus we begin with a clear admission that there may be reason to doubt the power and validity of conscience—that its present effectiveness appears questionable. The very fact that we can raise these questions makes discussion of the problem important.

We are guided by the historical realization that in the course of cultural evolution—and not only in the West—there is no phenomenon, apart from religious faith, which determines the character of an event, the quality of a work of art or an epoch, so much as conscience, not only through its power to stir us but through its failures. Whether we read the Greek tragedies, immerse ourselves in the world of Plato and Socrates, proceed from Saint Augustine and Dante to Shakespeare, Cervantes, and the dramas of the classical age in France and Germany, and then direct our attention to Dostoievski, Tolstoi, Kierke-

3

gaard, to Stifter or Gotthelf, we constantly find that, over and above its artistic merits, the universal validity of a work of poetry is conditioned by a deeper, mysterious power which enables it to remain alive and timely, generation after generation. Such timeless works are, above all else, embodiments of a moral attitude; through their protagonists they reveal a striving that in its innermost essence is an expression of what we call conscience. The conscience that dwells within them is what lends them imperishable immediacy.

If this is true in the domain of poetry and literature, it is true also in the sphere of political and social events. Though economic interests, dynastic aims, and power politics may dominate the scene, the great upheavals of nations, the decisive revolutions, are precipitated in the name of conscience. They aim at defending or asserting lofty human aspirations and socioethical demands. The groundswells of social movements are driven by the currents of conscience. And if morality only too often serves as a mask for baser, ethically doubtful purposes, the mask itself—the fact that it is meant to hide other designs—testifies to the authority of the ethical command and its hidden, inescapable effect.

It is this enigmatic power and its role in present-day life that we are compelled to ask about today. We ask because, with increasing frequency, we are beset by the uneasy feeling that conscience in our time has melted into thin air; and we are bound to note that this vitally important, primal, and most spiritual power and its spontaneous working are only too frequently absent from contemporary events or have grown feeble and dumb, when in the midst of the dangers that beset us we would like to hear its voice clearly and unmistakably rousing us to action.

Seventy-five years ago an event took place which shook the Western world and brought its conscience to the boiling point, driving men's minds out of their hiding places and complacency, passing through the nations of the West like an outcry: the Dreyfus trial in Paris. At that time the fate of an inconspicuous, indeed rather unsympathetic individual, wrongly condemned for high treason, still managed to launch a tremendous wave of indignation. Not only in France, but everywhere, the leading minds were stirred to their depths and divided into two camps, which rose up against each other in the name of justice and conscience. Zola's *J'accuse* was the signal for this revolt, as well as its voice. The world's conscience was aroused, and it was not allayed until outraged justice was restored and the higher conscience had achieved victory.

Two decades later the world's conscience again raised its voice, renewed by the words of a Frenchman, when Romain Rolland uttered his warning cry *Au-dessus de la mêlée,* and in Switzerland, when another poet, Carl Spitteler, emerging from his aristocratic reticence, professed his faith in the values of Western morality in his address *Unser Schweizer Standpunkt.*[1]

And since then? It is true that we have been strongly shaken on several occasions; for instance, during World War II, when an all too timid refugee policy in Switzerland, the United States, and elsewhere tended to sacrifice the demands of the heart and of conscience to reasons of state, or when the abominations of the concentration camps became known. In 1956 and as recently as 1968 our passions were aroused when the conscience of the world rebelled against the repression of peoples fighting for their freedom in Hungary and Czechoslovakia, though the world was unwilling to do more than remonstrate.

Has conscience in our age really become so paralyzed and dulled, so short-winded, that its impetus carries it for shorter and shorter distances, and then it crawls back again into its everyday shell of petty purposes and cares, knowing itself safely sheltered by comfort and economic prosperity?

---

1. Carl Spitteler, Nobel Prize laureate and well-known Swiss poet of the first part of this century, made the speech "Unser Schweizer Standpunkt" (Our Swiss Point of View) in December, 1914, at a time when the German- and French-speaking parts of Switzerland were at loggerheads over the issue of World War I. In disavowing nationalism and advocating European unity he lost his literary reputation in Germany. At the very same time Romain Rolland fell into disgrace with his French public for speaking out against French nationalism.

The world takes cognizance of injustice being done everywhere and all the time, protests are raised in parliaments and in newspaper articles, and then only too often everything goes again on its merry way. New sensations provide new excitement, until even the call of conscience is just another sensation of the day, like the warning issued by the eighteen German nuclear physicists and, shortly before that, Albert Schweitzer's appeal against the dangers of experimenting with atomic weapons.

We have become inured, it seems; and what is even more perturbing is the fact that we have apparently resigned ourselves to this lethargy. To improvise on Dostoievski's theme of the "unknown bacilli of unbelief," it is as though a mysterious virus had invaded our psychic organism, causing a moral paralysis that makes us increasingly incapable of recognizing injustice with sure instinct and of reacting against it with determination.

It is not the much-lamented "laxity of morals," the loosening of social ties, that we refer to here, not the moral emancipation, which makes itself so particularly felt among the young. Morals were often very free in earlier times, too, as in the autumn of the Middle Ages, in the Renaissance, during the *ancien régime* of the eighteenth century, and in the Rococo and Romantic ages; in reality, private morality was never very puritanical. Moreover, the easygoing attitudes of the younger generation and of our time in general, the loosening of certain restraints which many people anxiously and too simply interpret as "signs of moral decadence," are not to be judged only by their excesses. People are simply franker today. Perhaps there is less hypocrisy. And, to the extent that truthfulness and a sincerity that occasionally seems to border on cynicism are a part of all genuine morality, it may even be conjectured that, because we are more open, we are in certain respects even more moral now than in earlier times. Perhaps this explains why critical moralists since Nietzsche and modern critics like Bernanos, Thornton Wilder, Tennessee Williams, and Friedrich Dürrenmatt meet with such persistent and, for many people, liberating response, particularly among the young.

The forms of morality are changing; contemporary customs are less veiled, less constrained, showing without false modesty what was always there—if partially hidden and dissembled. It would be mistaken to assume that loyalty and faith no longer govern the everyday lives of most people and that integrity, decency, and honesty do not prevail.

Yet these are peripheral phenomena, mere superficial symptoms, which hardly touch the core of the problem. The problem becomes visible only when we abandon the narrow compass of private life, when we enter the realm of what, strictly speaking, may be called the conscience of the age—the world's conscience—where the personal sphere merges with the universal and where the major concerns of the whole community are at issue.

It is with this aspect of conscience in our time that we are concerned here. And this is where we see an ever deepening void stretching before us, a kind of no-man's-land which gives back no echo, in which the voice of conscience dies away without effect.

In discussing this problem in what follows, we should like to point out that our concern is not with any particular kind of conscience, although the Christian conscience of the West is the one with which, in the very nature of things, we are most familiar. In the course of historical development and in different cultures Christian conscience has, however, assimilated a variety of contents and forms, some of which will be discussed more closely in this symposium. Our primary concern is with the fundamental factor that is common to all these phenomena, which occur in various though essentially similar ways in non-Christian cultures also—and do so particularly dramatically and tragically where traditional ideals clash with the highly organized industrial and technological world of the West.

Today the intellect is more wide-awake than ever before;

reason is highly trained, technological and scientific activity is in full swing, the fever of industry and of organization mounts unceasingly; but seldom, it would seem, has what we call the voice of conscience within us been so timid, so dull, so toneless. Even though modern society is making unrelenting efforts for collective and social improvements, for the welfare of the masses, this livelier sense of social responsibility serves to relieve the conscience of individuals, indeed to lull it to sleep, because, as Renan has said, "organized egoism takes the place of charity."

We work ourselves up about the fate of the underdeveloped countries; we deride colonial imperialism; in our own eyes we appear very human and Christian and, in the anonymity and collectivity of mass organizations, which are steadily growing, along with their bureaucratic apparatus, we partially hide the dwindling of personal concern and the tepidity of our conscience.

The extent to which we have grown accustomed to diverting the impulse of conscience into the mainstream of anonymous institutions, associations, societies, and organizations is palpably revealed by one trifling symptom: the evaluation of a particular deed as a "courageous act." A clear, firm attitude of conscience has become so little a matter of course for us that we involuntarily feel a perfectly morally self-evident attitude —the reaction of a keen conscience—to be a sign of special courage. In a climate of general conformity, of weak compliance, not to say cowardice, any modest revolt of conscience appears exceptional, as courageous, arousing astonishment or admiration, at times almost embarrassment, and in many people shy dismay. Uninvolvement and detachment seem to have become the general norm.

II

FROM THIS CRITICAL, necessarily generalized picture of conscience in our time the suspicion arises that we may have succumbed to the temptation of an unduly pessimistic and unfair judgment in favor of a glorified vision of the past, as though, in enumerating its present characteristics, we wanted to insinuate from the start that in earlier times conscience made itself felt more passionately, more vigorously and resolutely. This is a moral pessimism whose somewhat monotonous refrain of well-meaning and respectable indignation sets the tone for many people today and is considered almost good form.

We would glorify the past unjustifiably if we were to assert that the power of conscience was pre-eminent at any particular period. What has come down to us from earlier times, what still grips us in the works of great poetry, in the lives of the saints, in the deeds of heroic men and women as the power of an inflexible conscience, have always been rare peaks sparsely distributed over long periods of time.

How the conscience of earlier generations acted in persons who were by no means average but belonged to an elite of the cultured classes may be illustrated by one small example taken from many similar cases. In the year 1675 the lower classes of Brittany rebelled against a new tax; the insurrection was suppressed with unprecedented cruelty, with all the drastic measures of which our rough-hewn forefathers were capable. An eyewitness of these atrocities reports them as follows in a letter:

> Do you wish to hear the news from Rennes? A tax of a hundred thousand crowns has been imposed upon the citizens; and if this sum is not produced within four-and-twenty-hours, it is to be doubled, and collected by the soldiers. They have cleared the houses and sent away the occupants of one of the great streets and forbidden anybody to receive them on pain of death; so that the poor wretches (old men, women near their confinement, and children included) may be seen wandering around and crying on their departure from this city, without knowing where to go, and without food or a place to lie in. Day before yesterday a fiddler was broken on the wheel for getting up a dance and stealing some stamped paper. He was quartered after death, and his limbs exposed at the four corners of the city. Sixty citizens have been thrown into prison, and the business of punishing them is to begin tomorrow. This province sets a fine example to the

others, teaching them above all that of respecting the governors and their wives, and of never throwing stones into their garden.

This was followed soon afterward by information communicated in a further letter to the same recipient:

> You talk very pleasantly about our miseries, but we are no longer so jaded with capital punishments; only one a week now, just to keep up appearances. It is true that hanging now seems to me quite a cooling entertainment. I have got a wholly new idea of justice since I have been in this region. Your galley-slaves seem to me a society of good people who have retired from the world in order to lead a quiet life.[2]

Madame de Sévigné, who wrote this to her daughter, the *gouvernante* of Provence, in the autumn of 1675, was anything but brutal by nature. She loved her children dearly and treated her tenants and servants with kindness. She was simply caught in the confines and outlook of her century and her class. Alexis de Tocqueville, quoting this passage, remarked:

> When the chroniclers of the Middle Ages, who all belonged to the aristocracy by birth or education, relate the tragic end of a noble, their grief flows apace; whereas they tell you at a breath and without wincing of massacres and tortures inflicted on the common sort of people. . . . In our time the harshest man, writing to the most insensible person of his acquaintance, would not venture to indulge in the cruel jocularity that I have quoted; and even if his own manners allowed him to do so, the manners of society at large would forbid it. Whence does this arise? Have we more sensibility than our fathers? I do not know that we have, but I am sure that our sensibility is extended to many more objects. . . . In democratic ages men rarely sacrifice themselves for one another, but they display general compassion for the members of the human race.[3]

2. Alexis de Tocqueville, *Democracy in America*, the Henry Reeve text as revised by Francis Bowen, now further corrected and edited with historical essay, editorial notes, and bibliographies by Phillips Bradley, 2 vols. (New York: Vintage Books, 1954), II, 174–75. Copyright © 1945 by Alfred A. Knopf, Inc. Permission to quote from this edition of de Tocqueville has been granted by Alfred A. Knopf, Inc.

3. *Ibid.*, pp. 173, 175–76.

Reading in the *Inferno* of the frightful retribution which the stern judge metes out to Dante's contemporaries and to earlier generations, we are appalled by the spectacle of brutality and lack of conscience that is revealed, even in men who were outstanding representatives of their age. Dante's poem is the vengeful judgment visited upon whole epochs in the name of an impassioned, solitary conscience. Yet his age is the very period which, in the bird's-eye perspective of history, appears to us as the Golden Age of faith, of cathedral-building piety. With his inner voice Dante stood alone in his time, like Francis of Assisi before him, like Socrates in antiquity, like the zealous prophets of the Old Testament, and like Kierkegaard in the nineteenth century or Nietzsche, the transvaluer of values and proclaimer of a new conscience.

A powerful, active, and clear-sighted conscience must have been rare at all times. This is proved by the fact that men who, undaunted, let the call of conscience ring out and who carried the fight to extremes in its name appeared as exceptions, not only to their contemporaries but to their descendants, who sensed in them something deeply stirring, as if they were moved by a higher power. The veneration they were accorded, partly in their own lifetime, partly later, was comparable only to the hatred they aroused in others. Would this be conceivable if the voice of conscience had been a matter of course in this world, if its call had been the norm or virtually the rule?

The fact is that people like Gandhi, Tolstoi, and Pascal, Teresa of Avila, Catherine of Siena, Bernard of Clairvaux, and our own Niklaus von der Flüe in Switzerland were universally felt to be exemplary proclaimers of the moral imperative, to be warning and admonishing witnesses. This should indicate to us that such incarnations of conscience, such fighters for justice, peace, and the dignity of man, have always been experienced as unique, almost legendary phenomena.

While we must guard against idealizing the past in comparison with the present, this does not mean that we can quietly brush aside the question of conscience in our time. On the contrary, today the problem is more acute than ever and urgently requires attention. For the current feeling of moral insufficiency is not simply one of a general—as it were, habitual —weakness of conscience, such as is inherent in our nature and noticeable in any epoch, with only the rare exceptions offering an inspiring contrast. Nor are we reassured by the statement that, by and large, morality is not noticeably less well or very much better observed nowadays than formerly and that general good will, sympathy, and social responsibility for human beings are actually more widespread in present everyday life than in earlier, harsher times.

The question is a different one. It arises from the radically altered social situation in which we have been placed by the development of modern science, technology, and industry.

III

WE LIVE IN AN EPOCH characterized by an unprecedented upsurge of material power, sustained by a universal dominance of intellectual and rational activity. Science, technology, industry, internationally organized, and trade organizations have during the past century and a half increased the material power of the Western nations to a degree unknown in any earlier culture.

Has our moral development kept pace with this? Or, to put it another way, do the moral order and power of our world correspond to the resources which are available for political, technological, and military purposes? Is our conscience on a par with the potentialities and dangers of atomic energy?

The anguish of conscience in our day has grown out of the disastrous shift in the ratio of forces—to the detriment of morality. Measuring it against the tremendous increase in material resources, we have to concede a dismaying lag in our ethical impulses.

Every epoch and society has institutions which embody its moral capital—its ethical energy—and through which it reaches the public. In antiquity it was the polis, later it was the Roman constitutional state; in the Middle Ages it was the church and the monastic and chivalric orders; and then, for awhile, it was the Holy Roman Empire. These were structures whose moral authority and power were proportionate to the existing means of material development. Often, of course, they would fail, betraying humanity, but they were always viable, authoritative, support-giving, balancing the external powers and aims of the state, the classes, the political and military leadership, and economic interests.

The fundamentally different and disquieting thing about our situation is the growing disproportion between outer progress in the Western world, its overwhelming material and technical resources, on the one hand, and the stagnation or insufficient advancement of the inner powers, particularly ethical ones, on the other.

This disproportion cannot be glossed over by the undeniable social improvements which have been made in so many areas, as in child welfare,[4] in the care given to the aged, the poor, and the sick, in short, in the great achievements of social welfare. These improvements do not touch the core of the situation; by somewhat different, i.e., organizational and legislative, means in an ever expanding field of work, they merely continue a long-established and necessary task.

In his famous formula *cogito, ergo sum,* which has now become the motto of the Western world, Descartes posited thinking and ratiocination as the true hallmark of human consciousness, as its coat of arms, so to speak, thus equating reason with spirit and proclaiming the primacy of the intellect. This doctrine has, ever since, undergone an unsuspected development and application. Seldom has a philosophical idea prevailed so triumphantly and so extensively.

Our whole epoch gives proof of the conquering, sovereign power of knowledge, of rational cognition and the way of life and organized existence founded upon it. But what has become of conscience, insight, and wisdom? And what about the au-

---

4. Initially child labor was abolished not for humanitarian but for military reasons, simply because it became apparent that exploitation at an early age noticeably reduced the quality of a soldier's service.

thority and effective influence of institutions which, as vehicles and guardians of the ethical imperative, would constitute an equally increased counterpoise to the development of external resources? What of the authority of organized religion, the moral standing of the state, of governments?

So our question about conscience in the present—and in time to come—is prompted by genuine concern as we view the ever widening gap between knowledge and conscience, between knowledge of nature and human insight, between domination of nature and mastery of the self, between technology and ethics, practical materialism and moral culture, the training in skills and the true education of the mind.

Why does the development of the impulses of conscience lag so far behind those of reason? Is *cogito, ergo sum* really the clue to human existence, the ultimate conclusion of knowledge? Prior to all thinking, to all conscious cognition, man lives in a community, beginning with the first relationship between mother and child. From there he grows into organic relatedness, which later, as loving and being loved, sustains not only all forms of fellowship but cognition as well. According to Dante, love moves the world, his hate-filled heart rising up purified to the kingdom of love, which appeared to him as the face of Beatrice in Paradise; and Leonardo da Vinci claimed that love is the mother of knowledge. In the great tradition of Platonic thinking, he was still aware of the meaning of living knowledge and the roots of all cognition, which later ages increasingly lost sight of, only to entangle themselves in an abstract conception of truth and a narrow, specialized knowledge, alienated from life.

Is not moral consciousness—*amo, ergo sum*—the true hallmark of the human mind? Is this not, in the profoundest sense, the true measure and value of man, that which distinguishes him from all other living organisms on earth?

IV

BEFORE WE PROCEED, let us say a few words about conscience itself and the forms it takes as a psychic phenomenon.

How does this peculiar power manifest itself in the human soul—this power which intervenes in our lives in a strangely irrational way? Sometimes it is peremptory, prodding; sometimes it is oppressive; again it is triumphant and liberating, then a torment, judging or condemning our desires and our deeds and seeking to guide them.

Above all, unlike a moral command, which is conceived in general, abstract forms, conscience always manifests itself concretely. It bears the features of the society, the epoch, and the tradition, as well as the environment, in which a man lives; furthermore, it expresses the personal makeup of the individual, mirroring in weakness or in victory that which is unique in his nature.

Conscience is thus collective and individual at once. That it bears the unmistakable traces of age-old evolution and conflict has been abundantly demonstrated by modern psychology, ethnology, and the psychology of the individual. Conscience is a hoard of archetypes. At the same time it exhibits unique features in each one of us; no man's conscience behaves exactly like another's, however uniform the contents may be. It appears as an inner voice, with the countenance of some religious figure, of a saint, of one's father, of someone venerated; it speaks with their words, admonishing and guiding.

At times it may be quite feeble in a man, barely stirring, the merest whisper; then again it may burst in upon him with passion, persecuting him, chastising; again it may fall mute, only to break forth threateningly once more. It can be a veritable torture, pursuing a man like the Erinyes, driving him to suicide, into madness, or rousing him up to some redeeming deed.

It is never an abstract, impersonal "You ought," and in this it differs from ethics, with which it is essentially in accord. But it can also run counter to ethical commands, and this conflict is one of the greatest dramas of conscience. For here conscience is not at one with itself; it cries out with two voices in us, each claiming to be the "right" conscience and making irreconcilable demands. An example of this would be the clash between a patriotic conscience, which in certain circumstances is a summons to military service, and the commandment "Thou shalt not kill." Again, the conscience of the family or tribe may come into conflict with aspirations that are contrary to its interests as a group but which argue in favor of the wider community.

Conscience may also assume forms that seem perverse to us. In the member of a band of criminals a kind of gang conscience may develop. The member of a gang stands by his fellows from an inner sense of duty; despotically ruled by it, he is inveigled into illegal actions. Then there is the conscience of a resistance fighter, who, at its behest, persecutes, tortures, and kills his own countrymen and suffers from a "bad" conscience if he fails to accomplish the murderous mission entrusted to him.

Then we meet with obstinate and dictatorial forms of conscience that ruthlessly and pitilessly demand obedience of themselves and others, and even self-destruction: the conscience of a Prinz von Homburg, a Michael Kohlhaas.[5] Other forms degenerate into a mania for litigation or take on the puritanical severity of an Old Testament, a Calvinistic, conscience.[6]

Sometimes a split occurs between the zealous, rigid, narrow-minded conscience of a sect and the striving for a nobler, freer humanity. The same conscience that makes a man into a champion of liberty and justice may suddenly turn him into a slave who—as under the Reign of Terror in the French Revo-

---

5. Heinrich von Kleist, "Michael Kohlhaas," *Sämtliche Werke und Briefe* (Munich: Carl Hauser Verlag, 1961), II, 9 ff.

6. Cf. the moral precepts by means of which the American Pilgrim communities of New England strait-laced their citizens into plated armor, so to speak, while at the same time creating one of the most independent, individualistic nations.

lution and in many other revolutions—rages against his own freedom and that of his fellow men. The pathology of conscience abounds in destructive contradictions of this kind, which always indicate a split of the personality.

One constant feature of conscience is its claim to unconditionality, even when it appears fragmented into two or more voices. This unconditionality also applies to people who think they can live a life "beyond good and evil." The Russian poet Saltykov tried to describe such an attempt at a life beyond good and evil in his tale entitled "The Lost Conscience." After having thrown off conscience, which had dwelt among them as an insignificant and useless phenomenon, the characters of this tale all seem to feel gloriously happy and relieved. Yet, in spite of their strenuous efforts to the contrary, conscience always comes back to one or the other; they try to get rid of it, to destroy it, but in vain, for a strange restlessness drives them again and again to search for it. Conscience cannot be removed from the surface of this earth; it is always there, in unexpected places, and cannot be lost.

All gradations and forms of conscience can be found in any given epoch or society. The conscience of an age is not a homogeneous thing, if we disregard its general contents; earlier evolutionary stages go on living in it, occasionally breaking through in force and overpowering subsequent, higher forms of behavior. In times of profound upheaval, as in wars and revolutions, we experience the tragedy of such conflicts of conscience in race hatred, chauvinism, and other manifestations of the atavistic stages of conscience.

Although molded by society, conscience is at the same time uniquely individual. We can speak of a "collective conscience" or "mass conscience" only in a figurative sense. Just as it does not possess a personal psyche of its own or its own reason, neither does the collective have its own specific conscience. What we assume to be the collective conscience is either the condensed expression of what is already alive in the individual consciences of the members of a group, a society, or a whole epoch, now become audible in monotonous unison, or it is the effect of the conscience of one or more men who stamp their conduct on others by suggestion and carry them along.

Conscience is surrounded by an aura of solitude as well as multitude, of ego as well as the world; and in the depths of consciousness, from which it arises, it makes contact with the hidden powers of the whole universe, of the eternal.[7]

Today we have the impression that conscience is more ready to succumb to alien suggestions, to adapt itself more willingly to collective slogans and opinions. Individuals seem increasingly inclined to submit to mass thinking and to repudiate the sovereignty of their own conscience. Readiness to conform has become more general, either because many people turn a deaf ear to their conscience or because its voice has grown fainter, more uncertain, weaker.

Now let us turn back to the question from which we started: the discrepancy between material and technological development, on the one hand, and the lagging of ethical forces, on the other.

V

WHAT CAUSES have produced the backwardness, the visibly decreasing potency of conscience in our time? Let us first single out a few. It is in the nature of conscience as a central power in the psyche to be influenced and molded by countless processes which play their part in our social and intellectual life. Nearly everything leaves its traces on conscience.

In a certain sense the century that brought the Cartesian primacy of reason to maturity came closer to a balance between intellect and conscience, between inner and outer development, than the two centuries that followed. Despite all the shortcomings of traditional institutions and the feudal system,

---

7. The inner drama of conscience in the form of a soliloquy, with conscience in the role of monitor and judge, has been extremely well illustrated in Holzapfel's psychological analyses ("Gewissen," *Panideal* [January, 1923], Vols. I and II). The writings dealing with this subject from the psychological and ethnological point of view in the light of Freud's and Jung's work are almost legion.

a balance existed in which the ethical attitudes of an elite were
not outweighed by its economic, military, and political resources. The ideals of the *honnête homme*, the *homme de bon
sens*, and the *gentleman*, which shaped the conscience of that
class and its leaders, were still able to counterbalance the
material powers in spite of the occasional brutality and cruelty
of custom and action.

The first serious inroads were made by the French Revolution. That sounds unexpected, almost paradoxical, accustomed
as we are to regard this event as the breakthrough of a new
humanitarian and liberal conscience. Yet the cataclysm that
destroyed the old order in the name of humanity's conscience
and human rights and sought to establish the equality and
fraternity of all men unleashed forces which time and again
were to imperil these very ideals. Nobody recognized this
more clearly than de Tocqueville.

The first of these forces burst upon the scene with Napo-
leon, who created a national army and with it waged a long
and successful fight against the old armies of mercenaries.
Equality made a soldier of every *citoyen;* thus the fatal web
was woven which increasingly involved the whole population
in national wars. In some armies, in Russia, Prussia, and to some
extent in Austria, the citizen-turned-soldier was degraded into
a slave, at the mercy of the brutal sergeant mentality; the aim
of military training was to break his will and make him a
robot-like tool of the war machine. As a consequence, the
personal attitude toward conscience also had its back bent, if
not broken. Men were trained to be servile subjects instead of
citizens. Even when the citizen was respected in the soldier and
he was not forced to surrender his human dignity, the afteref-
fects were not long in coming. Especially in wars of aggression
launched in the name of national glory and aggrandizement,
the majority of the citizens were a prey to fanaticism, which
filled them with hatred, contempt, and rage against the enemy
and indeed was bound to do so if they were to fight success-
fully. Psychological propaganda—the whipping-up of nationalism—now became an essential ingredient in the warfare of

democratic states. This ominous development, continued with remorseless logic and devastating consequences in the total war of the technological age, no longer makes any distinction between soldier and citizen. It grips all members of the populace, including noncombatants, body and soul. As a result of education for war, and owing to the manner in which war is conducted, neither women nor children, neither the old nor the wounded, are spared. The peasant peacefully ploughing between battling armies, as depicted in old miniatures, is swept away from the battlefronts; between opposing forces there is nothing but a desert of total annihilation.

The amalgamation of the nationalistic spirit of the people (not to be confused with the healthy stirrings of patriotism and love of one's homeland) with the belligerent aims of conquest and power has dealt modern man's moral sensibilities a disastrous blow, the effects of which have continued down the generations into so-called times of peace and have helped to entrench national prejudices, through poisoning and distorting the image nations have of one another.

This development culminated in the perfected barbarism of technological total war, with its ruthless destruction, its fight against whole peoples. In the face of total war humanitarian endeavors like the Red Cross, immunity for special areas for the civilian population, protection of artistic monuments, look like attempts to hold back a tidal wave with palm branches or wooden crosses. Technological advances have in turn accelerated and exacerbated this development.

One of the laws of total war is that the more ruthless opponent will finally force the more humane enemy to adopt his methods of fighting. This kind of cynicism has no doubt done much to blunt the moral sensibility of the masses, along with part of the ruling classes, and to spread a kind of fatalistic indifference, not only during wartime itself—perhaps there is less of it then—but, above all, in the aftermath of war.

This process is allied with a number of others which, in the past century and in this, have helped to undermine the authority of conscience and the belief in its effective power.

The most important of these factors is the decay of religion which followed in the wake of the rationalistic skepticism of the Enlightenment and the predominance of a positivistic and materialistic conception of science. If it was originally hoped that the utilitarian philosophical philanthropy typical of the eighteenth century would overcome the religious fanaticism that flared up during the Reformation, the Thirty Years' War, and the Inquisition, it soon became evident that the abandonment of the religious basis of conscience was to have even more disastrous consequences. In the long run, conscience, as historical and psychological experience shows, cannot thrive without religious roots. In time the decay of faith is followed by the decay of conscience. The connection between them is expressed by the word *religio,* which in Latin means not only "reverence for God" but also ethical consciousness. Ethical conduct can undoubtedly continue to be nourished for awhile by the juices of a vanished faith, just as some branches and leaves will go on flourishing for a time on an uprooted tree. Burckhardt and Gottfried Keller, despite their religious skepticism, continued to be deeply and firmly rooted in a Christian and humanistic ethic. A man like Ernst Abbe, creator of the Zeiss Foundation and a pioneer for social justice, was actuated by a powerful humanitarian conscience, although he was violently inimical to church and religion. Even in times when religious faith is weak the impetus of conscience will continue for awhile. History nevertheless teaches us that the decay of the religious world-image is inevitably followed by the moral collapse of a culture and often by its total decline unless the sources of faith, of the metaphysical relationship, are discovered anew. Whether this decline stems from the failure of our ethical and religious development to keep pace with scientific knowledge—from its adherence to views and forms which have embroiled it in ever graver contradictions with the scientific picture of the world—remains to be seen. Although faith and knowledge belong to two totally different realms of experience, the unity of the human psyche does not in the long run permit disharmony or disunion between the two, if only because in all knowledge there dwells a particle of faith and in all faith a bit of scientific knowledge and rational experience.

Whatever the cause, the loss of the religious power to believe, the growing skepticism and uncertainty in religious matters, have necessarily had repercussions on conscience, which is indissolubly bound up with religious traditions.

VI

LET US NOW TURN to some of the secular causes which have contributed to the weakening of conscience in the past two centuries. In general we can say that the democratization of society, with its ideal of equality, has had some unexpected and sometimes distressing consequences for the behavior of conscience. This may again seem paradoxical at first sight, because it is customary to attribute the growth and stability of democracy ultimately to the power of conscience and to the moral attitude of the citizen.

Theoretically this is undoubtedly true. But the actual development produced results that at times deviate widely from theory. Certainly the breaking-down of class barriers and class prejudices freed sympathy from its fetters, broadened its scope, and enhanced the sense for what is human, for human dignity in general, without distinction as to outward group characteristics based on race, color of skin, or ownership of property. Thus the foundations for a new feeling of solidarity were laid. But in becoming more diffused, sympathy naturally lost something of its intensity; it became more abstract, more uniform. It lost in depth and individuality what it gained in breadth and freedom. Equality is first of all a mathematical concept. Something of the inner emptiness, the numerically impersonal, that attaches to it was increasingly transferred to personal relationships.

Abolition of all social hierarchies—complete equality in the political and social sense—had an effect on conscience that extended far beyond the realm of politics and law. When man loses his sense for degrees of values, when there is no spiritual counterweight to the leveling tendencies in the form of a hierarchy of psychic values, where quantity, large numbers, and the majority decide the issues, then the sense for differences, for gradations of quality, gradually disappears in the spiritual realm as well. The result is a general adaptation to mediocrity, which, unless powerful counterforces appear, inevitably leads to an adjustment downward, a descent to more primitive levels.[8] With this process, which de Tocqueville clearly recognized and the dangers of which he insistently stressed, the surrender of the highest standards of duty sets in, particularly when these demand something that is contrary to the opinion of the average man, "the man in the street," the "public," or great majority.

This process of downward adjustment is accompanied by a barely noticeable adaptation of the dictates of conscience owing to the erroneous but nonetheless traditional view that the majority opinion is also the expression of what is morally right and spiritually binding. The practical requirements and decisions of the political order are again confused with those of conscience and the spirit. However much this tendency was opposed by convinced champions of freedom and humanity like Schiller, Burckhardt, Ibsen, Gotthelf, and many others, however strongly the value of the "sovereign power of the majority" was again and again held in check, the sheer weight of it nevertheless exercised a permanent influence on conscience. This development ends with the use of statistical polls of the supposed opinion of the majority as a yardstick for political action. Gallup replaces the conscience of statesmen, and the rest of conscience soon follows in the footsteps of the emasculated political conscience. This is where the dictatorship of mediocrity begins, which so easily prepares the ground for other types of dictatorships.

In valuing and acting, conscience is in its very essence an upward adaptation. It cannot be reconciled with the prevailing

---

8. Cf. Hans Zbinden, "Innere Gefahren der Demokratie," *Welt im Zwielicht* (Zurich: Artemis Verlag, 1951), pp. 32 ff.

downward assimilation (called "mass-mindedness" today), which egalitarian democracy, contrary to the ideas of its original proponents, has so often fostered in the masses and ruling classes alike.

We might also note that the almost inevitable readiness to compromise—a requisite of democracy—does not contribute to resoluteness of conscience, particularly when false compromises are reached from mere weakness and easy compliance or from guile in contrast to settlements reached from inner, honest insight. The clear light of conscience is dimmed; instead there is a habituation to half-truths which panders to indifference. To counterbalance its own dangers, democracy requires an especially keen and sure training of conscience. This has often been lacking. Nowhere is this lack more fateful than when clever compromises are made with the enemies of freedom. One imagines one has got rid of the enemy only to wake up one day as his slave.

No less paralyzing in its effects is the fact that, from the American and French revolutions to the Declaration of Human Rights at San Francisco in 1948, the emphasis has always been on human rights but scarcely ever on human duties. A proclamation of rights assuredly always includes corresponding duties, yet few people seem aware of this. They are easily accustomed to demanding; they loudly claim their rights; far less often do they remind themselves of the obligations these entail. When Ortega y Gasset says, "We recognize nobility by the demands we make of ourselves, by duties and not by rights," he is only varying the profound dictum of Saint Augustine, "Deo servire libertas," or, as Alexandre Vinet, the Swiss philosopher and critic, puts it, "C'est pour servir que nous sommes libres."

Human rights direct the eye of conscience in one direction only; when human rights are outraged, conscience is justifiably indignant. But it turns its back all too willingly on the idea of service, responsibility, obligation; these remain in the shade. Is not the decline in the spirit of service, in understanding of chivalrous ideals, a striking sign of the impoverishment of conscience in modern democratic society?

These tendencies are strengthened still further by the effects emanating from what one can call the ubiquity of the masses, from the constant presence and pressure of large numbers, which makes it more difficult for the individual to have confidence in the power of personal values and choices. He sees himself faced with huge anonymous organizations, national and international complexes, structures with an impersonal bureaucracy, and, above all, with the steadily growing power of the state. He loses the courage to act on his own. Instead of undertaking responsible action himself, he leaves it to the collective authorities, which oust and usurp the authority of the individual conscience.

The psychological effect of the mass mentality, to which the majority of people are exposed today, is continually being fanned by news reports in the press, radio, films, and television, which follow one another in rapid succession. The daily drumfire of news from all over the world, in which sensation-mongering naturally gives first place to everything that is exciting, amazing, threatening, or depressing, creates a distorted picture of humanity. The impression one gets is predominantly one of unhappiness, meanness, malice, and stupidity; in comparison the voice of reason, of insight, of trust in constructive forces is barely audible.

In the nineteenth century the doctrine of "evolutionary automatism" in social life, particularly in politics and economics, was one of the factors which contributed to the discouragement of conscience. Bentham and Comte, who fostered this view, had full confidence in the benign course of evolution, whose own momentum would carry it toward continual progress. This conviction was shared by the two so dissimilar siblings, early liberalism and Marxism. Liberals believed that a self-regulatory economy, operating through the free play of individual egoisms, would make it unnecessary for the individual to respond in terms of intervention or reaction to ethicoeconomic demands. "Evolution," an object of almost mystical veneration in the thinking of the nineteenth century, would by the very laws of its nature produce a balance and bring the cream to the top. The same fatalism regarding progress, only in the opposite direction, is found in the Marxist belief in the dialectics of social forces, from which the classless society would necessarily issue forth. Its faith in inevitable change, independent of human volition and insight, reinforced the same "continence of conscience"; if social and economic changes follow of themselves and human will and action are only a blind tool or at best an accelerating auxiliary, incapable of creative intervention, then the call for acts of conscience becomes superfluous. This belief in automatic changes obeying an *anankē*-like law of dialectics had in Hegel's philosophy a support of the highest authority. Asserting the "self-activation of the concept" and believing that elementary evolution would necessarily lead to the ascendancy of the spirit, it reduced the will for personal participation and for moral struggle. Thus the prophet of the self-realization of "objective spirit" unconsciously paved the way for the dethronement of conscience.

Fortunately, this doctrine of a self-activating "progress" beyond man's control—whether toward the flowering of a free economy or the classless welfare state—could not prevent the stirring of counterforces. In the liberal and socialist camps alike, social conscience intervened, energetically influencing and guiding social and political developments in logical contradiction to their own theories. Human nature and the vitality of individual conscience proved stronger than the fatalistic doctrine of the amoral automatism of social events.

There is another process in modern society that has made an even more substantial contribution toward weakening the creative forces of conscience. Economic conditions and technology, together with the democratization of society, have sucked people into more and more strenuous and ceaseless activity, inhibiting in many of them the power of reflection, the readiness to take thought. The resultant feelings of emptiness and perplexity have driven them to yet more indefatigable bustle. In this vicious circle the stirrings of conscience, which need for their strengthening a climate of quiet reflection, meditation, and concentrated thought, were bound to atrophy. De Tocqueville, with his keen vision, early recognized the dangers that accompanied the evolution of democracy:

> Men who live in democratic communities not only seldom indulge in meditation, but they naturally entertain very little esteem for it. A democratic state of society and democratic institutions keep the greater part of men in constant activity; and the habits of mind that are suited to an active life are not always suited to a contemplative one. . . . In the ages in which active life is the condition of almost everyone, men are generally led to attach an excessive value to the rapid bursts and superficial conceptions of the intellect, and on the other hand to undervalue unduly its slower and deeper labors.[9]

The hustle and bustle of our lives leaves very little room for the creative deed.

A further consequence of democratic thinking is that people in general have a less lofty conception of man than that which prevails in cultures with clearly defined hierarchies. The tendency is to picture him as an average type and to belittle, if not devalue, anyone or anything that is outstanding. The elite can scarcely be recognized. The proverbial "man in the street" dominates the scene; he is the criterion, the yardstick.[10]

In aristocratic societies conscience is active in a relatively circumscribed class. But it is generally guided by a nobler vision of man, of his task and his mission. De Tocqueville wrote:

> Aristocracies often commit very tyrannical and inhuman actions, but they rarely entertain groveling thoughts; and they show a kind of haughty contempt of little pleasures,

9. De Tocqueville, II, 44. The glorification of "action," the dogma of *action directe*, as preached by Georges Sorel much later, is only the logical continuation of this general tendency and its application to the social struggle. Ernst Jünger's *Arbeiter* is one of its latest offspring. At the same time, the concept of the deed became steadily more unrefined. "Action" is increasingly characterized by violence, by destructive acts with a contempt for all preliminaries, such as negotiation and discussion.

10. Zbinden, *Vermassung und Demokratie* (Bern: Herbert Lang, 1954), p. 10, with statements by Lowell, Bryce, Burkhardt, and Feller.

even while they indulge in them. The effect is to raise greatly the general pitch of society. In aristocratic ages vast ideas are commonly entertained of the dignity, the power, and the greatness of man. These opinions exert their influence on those who cultivate the sciences as well as on the rest of the community. They facilitate the natural impulse of the mind to the highest regions of thought, and they naturally prepare it to conceive a sublime, almost a divine love of truth.[11]

Although the idea of human dignity—so much talked about in modern democracies and so constantly appealed to—is more widespread, it has undeniably diminished in *élan* and grandeur. So far, a sense of the sublime has not been the strong point of leveled societies. Here, too, evolution does not seem to have kept pace with our higher aspirations; our picture of man and his tasks has not grown in proportion to the material resources at his disposal, for the good use of which he needs the guidance of an equally strong spiritual counterforce.

VII

ANOTHER THREAT to conscience that we shall mention concerns the devaluation of words, the dwindling of conscientiousness regarding the use of language. The hidden but close connection between the moral and "linguistic conscience" can hardly be overestimated.

Democratic governments incline to loquaciousness. A devaluation, a slurring and emasculation of words, is a concomitant of this loquaciousness, as it is a by-product of ideologies with their verbal adulterations. Further contributing factors are a certain kind of arbitrariness and verbal acrobatics, or sometimes coarse and vulgar language,[12] which deprive conscience of its physical substratum, as it were, i.e., of the word through which the voice of conscience speaks to us. Language and character, use of words, and human quality are always closely

11. De Tocqueville, II, 45–46.
12. Grossly exaggerated expressions are intended to invigorate the emasculated word in order to render it more effective: "terribly" beautiful, "fabulously" intelligent, "damn" good, etc.

interrelated. Thus depravation of the one is usually indicative of the other's decay, and each tends to exacerbate the other. Anarchy of language, diminished respect for the word, and devaluation of meaning are almost always signs of decadence. The relationship is very like that between the state of a country's economy and the value of its currency.

Between moral confusion and the disintegration of language there are connections which penetrate to the core of irrational consciousness, where conscience has its roots. Conscience cannot remain untouched by linguistic demoralization, just as its own debilitation manifests itself in a disintegration of the meaning of words, briefly, in linguistic barbarisms which render the word ineffective.

Human dignity cannot be separated from the ethos of language, just as the validity of the word is inseparable from its "response," i.e., its meaning, which is expressed in the formation of the word "responsibility." Wherever reverence for the basic human laws is on the decline, respect for the norms of language and the forces which determine its organic growth also withers away; this process may manifest itself in an impoverishing mania for oversimplification, which, as a result of a thoughtless eagerness to reform, irreverently interferes with the delicate and sensitive fabric, or in a tampering with the language through stilted arbitrariness so frequently found in avant-garde literature. Thus, not only the structure of meaningful language is threatened, but—and only a few people are aware of this—the very roots of conscience are affected.

Conscience has a language. It speaks. At times it whispers, at other times it cries out. What it says is influenced by the everyday, as well as by the artistic, language of the times. Whenever language loses its clarity, conscience also forfeits some of its power. Flat, worn-out words are blunt weapons for its use. This is why reverence for the word and education for a wide-awake and keen-eared sense of language are prerequisites for the formation of conscience. It is not difficult to assess the extent to which the extremely mechanical style of digests, the shabby language of magazines and newspapers, not to mention the carelessness of style in novels or most translations or the jargon of technical journals—"scientific language," so-called —encourage vagueness and triteness of language and thus indirectly contribute to the blurring and shallowness of experience and conscience.

Here too, then, the formation and strengthening of conscience which a more disciplined sense of language, a greater responsibility vis-à-vis the word, might bring about, is sadly lagging behind the tremendous progress made in scientific research, technology, and industry.

If we try to visualize all these influences—and many others could still be named—with their gnawing and emasculating effects on the modern conscience, we are hardly surprised by its present condition. In fact, we are tempted to admire the toughness of conscience, which has been able to withstand so many crushing onslaughts and has prevented us from being precipitated into an even greater moral crisis. We begin to see in it some kind of primeval drive to survive, which gives us hope but at the same time constitutes a warning.

VIII

As WE POINTED OUT at the beginning, forceful and decisive manifestations of the universal conscience have in fact always been rare. Only among the few or, to use that risky word, "the elite," has it manifested itself from time to time in order to stir people to the defense of the highest human values.

How are things with the elite of today, those who claim to feel the greatest call to assume responsibilities? Can there be an elite without a spirit of service, of utmost devotion? Among knightly generations the concept of service was still known, and this created a basis for selection into the elite.

Above all it would be erroneous to consider those who think they represent the elite as the true incarnation of a live and courageous conscience. If the so-called "leaders" of politics, the arts, and industry were to be considered the elite, it would be difficult to claim that these are the people who excel in forcefulness of conscience. In our day there is much talk about the "failure of the elite," and we tend to overlook the fact that, as a social entity, the so-called leading classes have in terms of their moral attitude always failed in situations which required a courageous attitude, a clear call of conscience, instinctively secure; they rarely behaved differently from the other social classes. The *trahison des clercs*, as Julien Benda called it, is a chronic, almost constitutional manifestation.

Even in the leading intellectual circles it has always been the individual, the rare bird, who would rise first and who then, followed by a few others, would initiate a more widespread movement within the select group, which might then go beyond it and occasionally bring about a turn of events.

After all, poisonous influences are no less detrimental to this class than to any other well-defined group; and since, in addition, they are endowed with greater talent in the art of expression and more energy and intelligence, the destructive forces can develop all the more effectively in them, side by side with the constructive ones. This class is thus usually characterized more by sharpness of irony, sarcasm, or skepticism than by the seriousness of true humor and by relieving kindness. Human kindness is hardly the rule among them. We therefore have to ask ourselves whether those who are recognized as members of today's leading classes are synonymous with the real elite. They are naturally convinced that they are, but they rarely prove it.

In terms of conscience and behavior this class has never been "leading" in the true sense of the word, even if it considered itself to be so. The leading class has always depended on the one, or perhaps two or three, among them who would leave the ranks at the decisive moment to act as rebels and disturbers of the peace, arousing and awakening the dull conscience of their contemporaries by a call to arms, irrespective of the fate that was often held in store for them by their own class in alliance with the masses—whether this was the cup of hemlock or a no less pernicious form of "moral" social persecution, defamation, or ostracism.

The leaders, the people of influence in the artistic, scientific, economic, and political worlds, are, only exceptionally, moral leaders as well. The mysterious power of the universal conscience has shown itself surprisingly indifferent to artistic and scientific ability, as well as political or practical efficiency; it may ally itself with great gifts of the mind, but it may also choose a totally different carrier and walk in strange bypaths.

Is it accidental that in literature and history the stirrers of conscience are frequently the "dumb ones," the "simpletons," the awkward and the unworldly, people who are neither clever nor gifted nor "notable" in the traditional sense? Parsifal and Don Quixote are examples; the world of saints, of great religious innovators is rich in figures like these, one of whom— Niklaus von der Flüe—preserved the Swiss confederates from deadly strife by his call to conscience. Dunant, who initiated the founding of the Red Cross, was not at all a brilliant mind. In our times Bernanos and Graham Greene have again called up the power of conscience of these singular, even ostracized figures. They are lonely people and are far from considering themselves as chosen ones. Quite on the contrary, like Francis of Assisi, like Theresa of Avila, like so many others, they often think of themselves as rejected and deserted by God. Bunyan, the author of *The Pilgrim's Progress*, which was put almost on a par with the Gospels in England, meekly suffered eleven years of undeserved imprisonment, convinced that he really had been unworthy.

Furthermore, we are today hardly in a position to speak of an elite if we mean a clearly defined class or separate social group. As a result of their achievements or way of life some isolated individuals tower above their contemporaries; but insofar as an elite presupposes the possession of common and binding standards and a certain consensus regarding lofty esthetic, religious, and ethical ideas which, in spite of the manifold directions they take and the ways in which they are realized, condense into a synthesis of aristocratic traits and manifest themselves in a *communio spiritualis*—in these terms it would be difficult to claim that such an elite exists in this day and age.

Moreover, science, a main field of intellectual activity, has with its increased emphasis on the training of purely technical faculties and minds further promoted a narrowing of conscience. It is in the nature of things that all human work should be specialized; it is not the technical specialty, however, but the weakness of conscience that is responsible for the compartmentalization of mind along with specialization, going as far as complete ivory-tower isolation from the basic problems and general requirements of the community. The specialist who is extremely conscientious in his own field of research and activity somehow feels exempt from the same kind of attitude outside his specialty. He considers himself incompetent to express an opinion on questions touching on society at large, on purely human conflicts and political crises. If a few of them do so—and here one thinks of Einstein, Bertrand Russell, and, more recently some of the nuclear scientists like Oppenheimer, Heisenberg, and Niels Bohr—the majority of their colleagues are inclined to look upon this activity as a risky transgression of scientific competence or even as naïve if not presumptuous.

However, even in the field of science some voices have been raised, calling on scientists to assume greater social and even political responsibilities. About thirty-five years ago the widely read English weekly *Nature* put forth such a call in a long series of issues published over a period of several years, quite insistently, as if it were anticipating the tremendous responsibilities which the founders and representatives of atomic research would be burdened with today; and fortunately the number of those who seem to approve and insist on these obligations of the scientist appears to be increasing. Even more than theologians and churchmen, biologists, physicists, and doctors, in brief, the natural scientists, are in the forefront of this movement, while, strangely enough and perhaps significantly, the historians, theologians, philologists, and even the lawyers and judges seem to be much more reticent.

This does not mean that those who are creative intellectually, the scholars or poets, must become involved in the day-to-day struggles; to a large measure this is always a matter of personal disposition, temperament, and many other factors. On the other hand, it is important to assume responsibility, to take a clear-cut, authoritative stand at decisive moments, so that the demands of conscience will obtain a hearing.[13]

IX

WE HAVE ESTABLISHED the undeniable disproportion which exists today between the development of the external, material forces and the inner, ethical ones. We have seen the influences which have been responsible for this stagnation, and in part even retrogression, in the course of the past century and a half.

Our survey brings into relief the duties and demands upon our times and upon ourselves. It is clear that we must overcome this lag by a decisive change, a change in our aspirations and in our behavior.

All transformation is initiated by thinking, by cognition. We must re-establish the balance between our material means and the ethical impulses. Unless we can keep step morally, we shall soon experience the bankruptcy of all human values and culture along with the inevitable collapse of welfare and security in the midst of all our economic and technological achievements.

There is only one way open to us, one to which the laws of civilized life must lead us. From the primacy of economics and technology, from the one-sided evolution of material power, we must return to the primacy of ethics as a guiding principle, requirement, and realization.

It would be senseless to fall into the trap of looking down on things material and technological. Their dynamism is as relent-

13. How miserably, for example, did the majority of German scholars, scientists, and professors fail during the "Third Reich"! Cf. Zbinden, *Ohnmacht der Eliten* (Zurich and Stuttgart: Artemis Verlag, 1965–66).

less as their achievements are necessary. But they must be subordinated to a power in the form of a spiritual world of values which carries us forward and guides us by an image of man which lights the way. For a long time this was *Homo faber*, and then it was *Homo sapiens;* at present both are insufficient. Today, with much more poignancy than ever before, we are concerned with the conception of *Homo humanus et religiosus*, with the man whose impulses of conscience are on a level with the great scientific and technological developments of the times and who by a deepening of faith also knows himself to be caught up in the powerful stream of eternity; as *Homo cosmicus* he rises out of Hell and Purgatory to become, like Dante, a wanderer among heavenly bodies.

A strange reversal has taken place. For thousands of years, even among the most primitive peoples, man related to the cosmos, to the heavens, frequently to the careless neglect of earthly matters. Today he reaches out into the cosmos by technological and scientific means, while he allows his relationship with the eternal, symbolized by the stars, to be stunted, selling himself to earthly concerns. Today the concept of matter has dissolved into that of energy, of a dynamic nuclear process. Yet, psychologically, man has made himself a prisoner of dead, dull matter, more avidly and stubbornly subjecting himself to it than ever before, although physical science has long since overcome this problem.

By strange detours our conscious mind is today led out of its partiality and narrowness back to where it really belongs; we might say that we have the material pointers to what should again become the spiritual path.

Keeping in mind the analogy of the revolutionary effects which the Copernican cosmology had upon the feelings and presentiments of the centuries that followed, there is one thing we can now affirm with certainty; whatever effects the new astrophysical and atomic image of the world may have on people's thinking, their outlook on life, and their imagination, *the new knowledge and its consequences for our social and cultural existence demand that we develop a more profound*

and active conscience. The most intelligent and clearest commentary that I read in the newspapers on the occasion of the
launching of the first earth satellite read as follows: "Toward
the starry skies above us our conscience has now been
summoned." [14]

By comparison with the material potential at our disposal
today, the backwardness of conscience cannot be overcome
rapidly. The new pace of change may, however, be accelerated
by the drama and the increasing gravity of the present situation.

In the history of civilizations, decisive transformations have
almost always been the result of dire necessity and fear, and
they were precipitated by pressures which had become unbearable, as if wrested out of the despair that comes from
torturing emptiness, an apparent dead end.

It is always thus that nations are spurred and driven forward.
Whatever cannot be achieved by means of instruction and
education, in the usual sense of the word, is finally brought
about, if at all (for the decline of a civilization is also possible),
by the old and ever present fateful question: To be or not to
be? If this saying has ever been justified, it is today. This we
know, and every day confirms it anew.

Thus the present situation, if understood properly, is an
appeal to our conscience. Clear recognition of moral apathy
and its causes is also the first prerequisite for countering it. It is
not fear as such, or the frustration of an alleged dead-end
street, which will decide the struggle. What is decisive is how
we respond to it, what we do with it. Furthermore, turns of
events are not brought about by the masses or by "general
trends" any more than by the elite. They are always the result
of a reaction that first occurs in a few individuals.

To strengthen conscience, we require faith in what the
individual can do if he really wants to do it. The widespread
unease over the emptiness into which one-sided, outward-di-
rected activity has plunged us goes a long way to preparing the

14. *Deutsche Zeitung,* Stuttgart, 1957.

ground for a more intensified search. There is no dearth of symptoms, of barely noticeable and yet significant signs which seem to point to a change.

Slowly, ever broader masses of the population sense the dreariness of an existence which exhausts itself in material affluence and which, in amassing possessions, loses sight of the one possession which alone can transform outer into inner impetus. Religious aspirations, the desire for a meaningful existence, are visibly on the increase. The realization that, with all our knowledge and skills, we are not educating people is spreading. Today we are gradually beginning to grasp the full import and the gravity of the things Leopardi, Hölderlin, and Pestalozzi recognized and imploringly asked for at the dawn of the age at whose zenith we now stand.

Of course, the symptoms which can be seen in numerous and often commonplace signs are still quite feeble. They are anything but an answer, and they are only the slow beginnings of change. But at least they betray the one thing on which everything depends and on which it is possible to build: the fact that it is impossible to smother ethical consciousness.

If the desire for freedom cannot be repressed in the long run —and the present has frequently corroborated this—neither can conscience be paralyzed or muzzled forever. Would we be speaking of a "moral crisis" if it were otherwise? Conscience may be silenced over long periods of time; it may be blunted, overpowered by meanness, injustice, brutishness, and dehumanization. It may become a discouraged or a chronically bad conscience; it may try to hide under the cover of ideologies or may seek support in any movement which might be a substitute for faith. It may seek refuge in the routine of daily work, in activities, or in the anaesthetizing distractions of a helpless and empty *dolce far niente*. But it does not allow itself to be permanently shackled and misguided. And even in the form of a "bad conscience" it does its duty, namely, where it acts as a thorn, awakening people and spurring them on to what must be done.

At a time of approaching historical upheavals Goethe put

the following words in the mouth of the Princess in *Torquato Tasso:*

> Ganz leise spricht ein Gott in unsrer Brust,
> Ganz leise, ganz vernehmlich, zeigt uns an,
> Was zu ergreifen ist und was zu fliehn.[15]
>
> (III. ii. 16–18)

Few things are more revealing of the present-day longing for a clear and strong power of conscience than the admiration —across national and continental frontiers—in which men are held who, in the midst of our threatened world, embody this conscience modestly, with simplicity and grandeur—men like Pestalozzi and, more recently, Gandhi, Einstein, and Albert Schweitzer. By doing their daily duties with compelling simplicity, convincing earnestness, and unerring clarity they carried out the calling to which their inner voice summoned them.

Those who stand up unexpectedly, at times and in places where no one would have expected them to do so, are always few and far between. Such voices in the wilderness might, however, be likened—and this should give us some hope—to certain colors of which only a few grains are required to color great quantities of liquids. In cases such as these a single person is as powerful as an entire nation. These admonishers may not always be able to provide the solutions, but they do prepare the ground for them. Maybe we are inclined to believe that in our own day it is incomparably more difficult to help conscience to a hearing and a breakthrough, thinking that for this reason its voice is now more feeble. We are wrong. It has been difficult at all times, for the issue has always been crucial, a struggle between life and death, and has usually taken place under circumstances which seemed hopeless. Today's situation is no different. However, it is up to us to listen to those few.

If we do not ignore the soft stirrings of our times, it might

---

15. "A God doth whisper softly in our breast, / Softly, yet audibly, doth counsel us, / Both what we ought to seek and what to shun" (trans. Anna Swanwick, *Dramatic Works of Goethe* [London: Bell & Daldy, 1871], p. 267).

not be too presumptuous to think that out of our troubled present the forces of a strengthening ethos, the cells of an elite which merits the name, might grow to maturity: an elite in whom knowledge and skill might combine with an unshakable power of conscience. To prepare the way, to plough the ground for this kind of aristocracy, is the task of our epoch, the supreme goal of those who are aware of their responsibilities. The summons is issued to all.

During the harassing years of tremendous upheavals, on the threshold of an even more hard-pressed epoch which was to become ours, Eichendorff wrote his profession of "Aristocracy and Revolution." In the pensive mind of this noble of a dying age, who deals mercilessly with the old aristocracy, the vision of an eternal nobility is conceived:

> For nobility, being essentially immortal, is the ideal element of society; it has the task of chivalrously preserving everything that is great, noble, and beautiful, wherever and however it might manifest itself, even in the common people, of reconciling that which is forever changing and new with that which is forever lasting, thus rendering it truly vital.[16]

16. Joseph von Eichendorff, "Der Adel und die Revolution," *Werke* (Zurich: Atlantis Verlag, 1945), p. 560.

Conscience
in Economic Life

Eugen Böhler

Translated by Ruth Horine

FROM THE PERSPECTIVE of science, politics, and everyday experience, it would seem unlikely, at first sight, that conscience has any place in economic life.

THE INEXORABLE LAW OF ECONOMICS

WITH THE PUBLICATION of Adam Smith's *The Wealth of Nations* in the second half of the eighteenth century, economics broke away from moral philosophy. Having discovered the existence of apparently inexorable laws of its own, which seemed to operate independently of ethics as well as politics, economics proclaimed its complete autonomy vis-à-vis all other realms of human culture. The concept of autonomy emerges even more clearly in Marxist thought, which regards the economic situation as the inevitable result of the conditions of production and which, in its materialist view of history, holds that human consciousness is a mere reflex of the economic base underlying it. Thus the attempt is made to prove that the evolution from capitalism to socialism conforms to natural law.

Political economists seemed to be equally unequivocal as regards the overriding importance of economic laws. Ultimately the fundamental idea of the eighteenth century—that only complete freedom for the individual could guarantee social harmony—led to the belief that only a completely free

43

economy would ensure the greatest good of the greatest number. Although certain elements of social welfare have been built into the structure of the market economy during the past several decades, the basic thesis continues to be upheld that economics must be allowed to operate in complete independence of politics and ethics if a maximum of welfare is to be attained.

The concept of the autonomy of economic laws would appear to have been confirmed, during the past few centuries, by the experience that economic motivations do indeed seem to be the main principle governing human conduct. Not only have economic questions been given priority over all other problems in matters of domestic and foreign policy, but economic gain has become the decisive yardstick in everyday life and the most important criterion for our entire educational system. Increased economic productivity has become the primary objective of society on both sides of the Iron Curtain. Against this, other considerations, such as personal ethics, health, and the protection of natural resources, can no longer prevail. The economic apparatus, i.e., the means of production and the social organization, has become thoroughly objectified, developing according to an inner logic of its own, and the result is that the human being is turned into its subservient slave.

THE ETHICAL REACTION

THE GROWING DOMINANCE of the economic apparatus called forth a corresponding protest. Beginning with Rousseau's call for a return to nature, the protest was further developed, first in the French Revolution with the "Rights of Man" and later with the Marxist notion of the "leap from the realm of necessity into the realm of freedom." [1] It has found modern expression in the popular-front thesis of the "forgotten man" as well

1. Friedrich Engels, *Herr Eugen Dühring's Revolution in Science* (*Anti-Dühring*) (New York: International Publishers, 1966), p. 310.

as in numerous moral movements intended to influence the social elite.

For reasons which will be explained later, the protest movement has, however, been unable to modify either the autonomy of the establishment or the growing power of the economy and the state. While the social critics have traced the causes of man's inhumanity to man back to the economic and social system, the power of the establishment has in fact proved to be even greater in the now existing Marxist societies than elsewhere. Another result has been a bad conscience of the ruling classes because they have been made the target of socioethical criticism by the lower classes. Under the influence of Christian thought the ruling classes have been led to believe that economics, like affairs of state, should be governed by ethical considerations; this belief has created an obvious situation of conflict in both areas, a contradiction between the ideal and reality, tending to split off the individual from society. This problem is in urgent need of clarification. The central difficulty seems to consist in how to render unto God that which is God's and unto Caesar that which is Caesar's. On this, even Jesus avoided giving a concrete or generally valid answer! It is therefore hardly surprising that each of the various creeds has attempted to deal with the problem in its own way. Some have done so by developing an extremely complex casuistry, while others have referred the individual to his personal conscience. This leads us to consider what the nature of this conscience might be.

THE NATURE OF CONSCIENCE

CONSCIENCE is an extremely complex phenomenon with many attributes and stages of development which have to be differentiated from one another. Human thinking through the ages, as well as our own experience and reflections, might lead us to describe it as a universal moral sense residing in the soul. It implies a sense of balance and wholeness, which can also be considered as the sum of human moral experience.

We might then define conscience as an authentic "awareness of the self" which makes decisions with regard to values. Good and evil are its chief concerns. It contrasts with "ego consciousness," which makes decisions about the usefulness of actions, i.e., about their cleverness or stupidity. It is significant that, ever since the eighteenth century, aphorists have been saying that modern man is more embarrassed when he acts stupidly than when he acts badly.

Furthermore, we must differentiate between a subjective level of conscience, which is what we usually have in mind, and an objective level. Here not only the archetypes come into play, but also phenomena such as the will of the people and public opinion, which today, however, represent extremely diluted forms of conscience.

Finally, it is evident that there are different layers of conscience, such as the biological layer, the collective unconscious, the personal unconscious, and the conscious layer. The fact that there are these layers implies that conscience is characterized by the same sort of contradictions as the psyche in general and that we can consider it as a unity only to a limited extent. It might best be described as a federal state in which various authorities are at loggerheads. We must then expect of it the same tendency to fragmentation that we observe in the psyche as a whole.

The evolution of conscience has taken place along two parallel lines. On the one hand, we have witnessed a universal historical evolution from collective coercion to personal responsibility. This development has been the direct result of the gradual evolution of consciousness, which took on very different forms in different individuals and peoples. On the other hand, the individual has experienced an expansion of his horizons of responsibility because he has become more aware of his unconscious processes, though we must admit that this has been more true in theory than in fact.

Both developments have been disturbed by man's alienation from his instincts. For this reason the tendency to develop a personal conscience and to achieve conscious realization has not led to greater security for the individual. It is in the very nature of things that the more recently developed aspects of conscience should be more unstable than the older ones when there is a separation of consciousness from the instincts.

The most important aspects of conscience have remained unconscious. The result is that among the vast majority of ordinary people it has acquired the authoritarian character of compulsion, so far as it is still operative at all, while in people with intellectual aspirations it has simply been watered down. The over-all result has been a growing insecurity in respect of ethical values.

It now remains to demonstrate the validity of these statements for the field of economics.

Conscience in Economic Life

I am inclined to believe that the biological and collective-unconscious layers of conscience, as well as the fragmentation of the psyche, are nowhere more pronounced than in economic life—with the possible exception of sexuality.

The overwhelming role assigned to the economy in our civilization seems largely due to the fact that the most important impetus for the acquisition of goods derives from such biological spheres as hunger, insecurity, and fear of destitution. The thinking of most people still appears to be mainly concerned with the struggle for self-preservation, permeated though it has been by concerns for secondary needs.

In the same category belong such phenomena as fear of economic crisis and negative attitudes toward luxury, as well as distrust of the durability of wealth and happiness. These attitudes, though belittled by modern rationalism, do not simply represent an instinctive awareness of the irrational "counterforce" that is associated with all of man's rational aspirations. They rather express man's instinctive fear of the degeneration which experience links with wealth and good living.

The reaction of the people against excessive contrasts between wealth and poverty or against relative positions of power, as well as egalitarian thinking in general, also have to be considered as emanations of the biological conscience. The political movements in which these reactions have found expression clearly indicate that certain economic conditions, rational as they may seem, are incompatible with the basic instinctual structure of man. Such conditions will give rise to irrational counterforces which endanger the entire economic and social system. The difficulties in which present-day financial policies find themselves may be traced to similar causes. It is here that "lack of conscience" has been most blatantly obvious.

Modern acquisitiveness, on the other hand, is a complex psychological phenomenon in which instinctive and rational factors and materialist and spiritual, egotistic and altruistic, motives are inextricably interwoven. But it would seem that the great importance which modern man—whatever his color or creed—attaches to economic considerations and the pre-eminence of the economic principle in all human activity are, at root, biologically conditioned. The economic value of things, their market price, also expresses their collective vital and existential value, which enters into the decision-making process in all other spheres as well.

Nonetheless, economic values and considerations must not be looked upon as unequivocal, absolute, or mandatory because of the importance they assume in life, although only too frequently this is exactly what happens. Even the instincts can err, and they can degenerate. In any case, man should be able to assimilate and integrate them into his conscious system of values.

And indeed, the economic factor is overemphasized largely because the instincts continue to operate uncontrolled by consciousness, although the economic conditions which gave rise to them have radically altered. Hence unreflecting people find themselves under a sort of biological compulsion to make use of all the technical and economic facilities which increased wealth makes available to them. This they do without regard for the long-range effects on themselves or on society as a whole. As a result, we indulge in international competition in the uses of atomic energy without thought for the consequences, and we possess accelerated means of communication without making proper use of the additional leisure time that they may have helped to provide. Medical and pharmaceutical palliatives are applied without due regard for the possibilities of long-term tolerance. Knowledge is continually being expanded regardless of man's ability to absorb it. Finally, there is the indiscriminate increase in consumer goods coupled with constant reduction of our capacity for enjoyment, our vitality, our creativity, and our personal freedom. This trend has gone so far that modern man is not even aware that it constitutes a problem, and he believes that he should be able to satisfy all his desires without feeling bored and to achieve progress without having to make sacrifices.

Similarly, biological fear in face of the constant threat of annihilation drives man to arm himself against all eventualities and to amass a maximum of wealth, power, and prestige, which the majority of people are never in a position to use. To a large extent the economy is devoted to the accumulation of goods destined for temporary gratification—stockpiles that are never used for the purpose for which they were intended.

We thus allow our instincts to function in exactly the same way in times of plenty that we would in times of need or of threats to survival. This threat may, of course, again become an acute issue at any time because of the tremendous population explosion in the underdeveloped areas of the world.

Lack of unity in our economic conscience and in our entire moral consciousness is a close corollary of this biological determinism. Our complicated technological and organizational machinery has tended to dissociate output from consumption. Any significant comparison between sacrifice and utility has, therefore, become impossible. This is undoubtedly the reason for the overemphasis on acquisition as compared with creative activity and for the extreme rationalization of production despite the irrationality of consumption. Although the satisfaction of man's hunger should be only a means to his creative activity, the instinctual orientation of the economy has made heightened economic productivity an end in itself, to which all other considerations must be subordinated. To amass a maximum of goods, man has had to conform wholly to the demands of technology and managerial considerations; he is thus compelled to forego the use of all his psychic resources except the intellect. Even the intellect is abused through over-specialization, and too frequently its creative potentialities remain untapped. In addition, professional activities and industrial occupations, coupled with urban living, tend to alienate man from his instincts. But he experiences real satisfaction only from the activation of these. It is no wonder that the long-range goal of the masses is to be freed from work to the maximum extent possible.

Yet, with this attitude, man tends to forfeit his happiness more than ever. Since professional work has become merely a means to an end and no longer carries with it any intrinsic satisfaction, people lack the proper motivation for the mobilization of all their energies and for identification with reality. During leisure hours the ungratified instincts seek an outlet in hobbies, which have become the great craze of dissatisfied collective man. But this does not rid him of his discontent, because the hobby cannot claim all his creative energy and it destroys respect for the highest values. In general, it amounts only to intellectual dilettantism and might be placed on the same level as the solving of crossword puzzles. At the same time, he has lost the capacity for easy, nonpurposeful play.

Modern individualism would have us believe that the fullness of freedom for man consists in his freedom to do what he pleases. But this is not so. Freedom means the release of creative energies for worthwhile tasks and presupposes that man has available to him the kind of work that would mobilize these energies. Furthermore, to be motivated to tap his psychic resources, man needs to be challenged to defend this freedom against external or internal coercion, as well as troubles and difficulties. In the absence of this compelling motivation people are in danger of becoming mere beneficiaries of luxury and wealth, indulging in the purely passive enjoyment of technological progress and of prosperity. We have an urge to use all our psychic resources. If they are allowed to lie fallow, they degenerate and turn against the social order.

This is why the one-sided rationalization of production contrasts so sharply with the irrationality of consumption. Among the psychological functions, emotional forces such as feeling, sensation, and intuition, which constitute the true cultural heritage of mankind, are not needed in a profit-making economy. In fact, they are considered to be inferior, and so they remain primitive. Human ability to evaluate, which is the basis for any economic conscience, remains underdeveloped. On the one hand, we are no longer able to weigh personal sacrifice against the fruits of our labor; on the other, it has become impossible to elaborate a personal and ethical scale of values to determine our real needs, which is borne out very clearly by our barbarous consumer habits.

This tendency is reinforced by another characteristic of the modern economic conscience, namely, the passivity of the evaluating person. As the economic and political apparatus grows in complexity, the influence which the individual can exert becomes increasingly insignificant. There is less and less incentive for him to demonstrate his personal initiative, his moral judgment, and, therefore, his conscience. Practically all decisions are made by collective authorities. They wield the political and economic power, against which the individual is helpless. The same authorities set up collective standards to which the individual in general conforms, offering no resistance so long as his livelihood is guaranteed. This state of affairs has assumed such proportions that modern man obtains not only his consumer goods from the large retail business organizations but also his cultural values. Needs and sacrifices are, therefore, evaluated almost entirely on a collective basis. In general, the individual does not even have the opportunity to develop tastes or needs of his own. He no longer takes an active part in the valuation process and accepts impersonal standards.

Personal choice between ends and means becomes totally impossible, since choices can be made only on the basis of ethical freedom. For this reason collective man meets his requirements not from inner need but in order to please or impress his fellow human beings. Inevitably he becomes the victim of publicity and propaganda, thus forfeiting any personal influence. The so-called individualism involved in the choice of car models or fashion creations does not really express a personal or individualistic attitude. It is merely a collective response.

Professional specialization of the evaluating persons and the attempt to set "objective standards" on the basis of an intellectual approach further reinforce this development. The time has come when an individual can no longer consider a given question from all points of view and elaborate a personal scale of values. In considering such questions as the size of an establishment, for instance, he makes decisions purely on the basis of the financial advantage to himself or to the consumer. The fact that such decisions may also affect the political fate of mankind or touch upon the problem of dictatorship by collective authorities versus personal freedom is passed over in silence by those immediately interested. They do not wish to complicate their practical decisions, and the narrow economic viewpoint thus becomes paramount. Imperceptibly it slips into the role of the highest and most real value, although ethically it is never more than a partial one.

The compartmentalization of intellectual thought which has led to the separation of politics, economics, ethics, culture, and so forth has had similar effects. Each one of these fields has developed apparently absolute principles with claims to autonomous validity. On the purely theoretical level this is quite justified, because here we are dealing with independent principles. On the practical level they must, however, achieve some sort of synthesis and not a mere compromise. This synthesis ought to be brought about by the individual; but since he plays an increasingly unimportant role in modern life, he lacks the personal scale of values needed for this purpose. In the end, a balancing of the various principles is achieved by mass shifts of collective values, which are inevitably associated with revolutionary upheavals, to wit, the current controversy between the economic and social-welfare viewpoints or the conflict between military and national priorities. All these struggles are carried on by means of abstract arguments which do not commit anyone personally. The individual is not even called upon to express a personal opinion in terms of a scale of values consciously thought through or, even better, arrived at by experience. It is therefore not surprising that his conscience lacks coherence and that he becomes a pawn in the struggle between abstract ideologies which destroy the very core of his conscience. Personal ideals cease to be cultivated, and the individual is no longer stimulated into giving proof of his ability to pronounce ethical value judgments. The end result is usually failure and degeneration of the instincts.

Finally, our present-day economic conscience suffers from the progressive narrowing of the individual conscience—in other words, a lowering of the standards to which the self-aware conscience can refer. This is possibly the most striking characteristic, because it is not what we would expect. Our intellectual life is characterized by a constant expansion of consciousness, and one could assume that conscience, too, would expand, especially since ours is said to be the "social welfare age."

That a progressive narrowing of the individual conscience has in fact taken place is due to a variety of circumstances. One of them is the splitting-off of the unconscious. Another is the expansion of collective ethics at the expense of personal ones. As the power of the establishment grows, invading the sphere of the individual more and more, and as people become more and more isolated, social cohesion and coexistence must be increasingly regulated by outer, "objective" standards. Impersonal order and regulations replace inner, personal discipline; compulsion supplants voluntary effort; and collective ethics crowds out personal values. In other words, responsibility is shifted from the individual to the group. The individual is only required to conform to external rules, while his personal conscience is more and more neglected and therefore atrophies. Although social principles have become increasingly important in our society, the individual's social attitudes, his obligations toward his fellow human beings and toward the community, are weakened. Conformism is today so compelling that it has reinforced the aggressive instincts of man. This has led to widespread latent as well as actual criminality, as the growing popularity of detective stories and "Westerns" demonstrates. It is undoubtedly the explanation of Lao-tse's saying, according to which expediency (i.e., collective rules for social conduct) is "the mere shadow of what is right and true and is portentous of confusion."[2]

As a parallel development to the withering of the personal conscience, we have witnessed the displacement of the inner world of feeling and emotion by the outer world of practicality and purposefulness. The rational element, which was once inseparably associated with valuation in the emotional processes, has made itself entirely independent in the scientific approach to economics, ethics, politics, and psychology. Science takes pride today in having stripped itself of all value judgments. Since the values of each of these fields are, however, intimately connected with the ethical context of human life and society, as well as with the moral conscience, the individual has inevitably been impoverished. Naked and rational self-interest, aided and abetted by technology, economics, the state, and the establishment, has become virtually the only aim in life that the individual wishes to pursue. On the other hand, together with his instincts and his conscience, man has altogether lost his cosmic continuity; and in losing his sense of values, he has fallen out of contact with his fellow men and with the cultural heritage of the human species. From having been a living circle, man has shrunk to a point of self-interest where economic or political calculation takes the place of

2. Lao-Tse, *The Simple Way*, trans. Walter Gorn Old (London: William Rider, 1913), Aphorism 38.

conscience. As reason has succeeded in penetrating ever more deeply into the mysteries of the universe around us, the space assigned to conscience has been reduced to a minimum, and it has been relegated to the lowest possible level. Knowledge and conscience have thus become polar opposites, and it is this cleavage that characterizes the current crisis of mankind.

IDEOLOGY AS A SUBSTITUTE FOR CONSCIENCE

EVEN THOUGH conscience has fallen into disuse as a positive factor, it continues to function negatively, i.e., in the form of the "bad" conscience. The contemporary intellectual is ashamed of his betrayal of human cultural values. He seems to have an uncanny feeling that somehow he may have figured things out wrong, that the weights in the scales may not be true. All that anyone seems to expect from anyone else is efficiency and performance; no one is ready to reciprocate, to make a "sacrifice," i.e., to do something for its intrinsic value. The result is that everyone distrusts everyone else. If, indeed, everyone withdraws to his own rational point of self-interest, then the ethical world is atomized. And atoms move according to the laws of nature, not according to the laws of ethics! This is the cause of our spiritual and mental fragmentation, for the legions of mutually exclusive concepts and opposing points of view without common standards. It is also the reason behind the call for common and sustaining ideas to bridge all contradictions, for humanism, for a united Europe, for human rights to protect wolf against wolf. It is the reason for the need to camouflage vested interests by putting up a moral façade. This is why modern ideologies, fruits of our degenerated conscience, are bastards when seen from the viewpoint of ethics. They are the offspring of shame and aggression, whose conjunction begot individualism and collectivism as twins with this in common: they are nihilistic, lacking in objective value criteria. The only difference between them is that individualism considers the individual as an end in himself, while for collectivism it is the community. Natural liberty, the great god of individualism, is undoubtedly most valuable; but, like wealth, it is only a means to an end. It destroys itself when it is not supplemented and ennobled by ethical liberty, without which we fall prey to our drives, our profit-seeking, our striving for prestige and personal recognition, and our social prejudices. Thus individualism deteriorates into mere collective behavior governed by collective standards. Instead of inner freedom and independence, social position, "pull," prestige, and the make and model of one's car become the be-all and end-all. Man thus becomes dependent on his instincts and the machinery which can gratify them: the state, technology, the economy, and science. Further, this kind of individualism alienates man from his fellow men, from nature, and from the divine. Dependence on the machinery of civilization is only a step removed from collectivism, whose highest value is the material culture and the collective institutions serving it. The mutation of individualism into collectivism is in full swing, being at the moment a democratic form of collectivism.

Gradually, institutional authorities of various kinds have simply taken over the guidance and organization of human development. Military technology increasingly determines the formation of states and enforces political and economic concentration. Within individual countries the techniques of communication and industrial production are coming more and more to govern the life of the individual. Psychological needs are almost entirely subordinated to the exigencies of increased productivity and the passive enjoyment of growing amounts of consumer goods.

It is by means of ideology that the objective powers of the cultural establishment are able to mold man, permeating him with collective standards. In this way the struggle of interests replaces the struggle of ideas. Organization is expected to achieve a sort of mechanical equilibrium; but this is impossible, because values and, therefore, conscience are no longer in a position to function as regulators. The socioethical problems of humanity—the problems of world peace, social justice, fiscal policy, and justice in general—have become insoluble because they are no longer related to the world of values and conscience.

Rational Ethics and Collective Ethics as Attempted Solutions

Two TRENDS OF THOUGHT have arisen to fill the vacuum created by the loss of conscience: rational ethics and collective ethics. Upon closer examination we shall find that they are intimately related. Kant, with his Categorical Imperative, may be considered as the founder of modern rational ethics: "Act only according to that maxim by which you can at the same time will that it should become a universal law." [3] The Categorical Imperative is an attempt to replace conscience by the axioms of reason. The end result of this attempt is the well-known welfare principle, the aim of which is to achieve the greatest good and progress for the greatest number, ethics assigning to this principle the same role that the theory of knowledge assigns to the principle of causality.

The error of this approach lies in the fact that it is purely formalistic and therefore remains ambiguous despite its unconditional formulation, or perhaps because of it. Even if one realizes that objective principles are inextricably linked with the subjective foundations of feeling, the error is not removed. This attempt leads either to pure conformism or to hopeless casuistry. Consciousness is permanently split away from reality, although it is reality which creates the conscious contents to which those principles are supposed to apply. Thus it is not surprising that, in the end, ethical rationalism leads to utter relativism. Rational principles cannot, therefore, replace conscience.

Along the same lines, the Marxists have attempted to replace conscience with sociological standards. They postulate that

3. Immanuel Kant, *Grundlegung zur Metaphysik der Sitten* (1st ed., 1783), p. 52.

ethical values can be realized by changing the economic and social order. Concepts like the "common good" or the "interests of society" are just as formalistic as the so-called welfare principle. In fact, they merely represent a political variant of this principle. In our view, individual conduct cannot be derived from the highest principles by either deduction or subsumption. On the contrary, conduct results either from the political struggle in which the individual is involved or from the influence of power on him. Usually it is some combination of both. In either case, conduct remains tied to the instincts, and ethics consists in superficial conformism to collective rules of conduct.

On the other hand, it has to be admitted that there are pertinent sociological explanations for collectivization. Collectivization will progress at the same rate and to the same extent that conscience regresses. Extreme individualism leads inevitably to the disintegration of society and to a growing differentiation of opinions, thus impeding the rational approach to decision-making. Political propaganda, or even political coercion, replaces the voluntary association of individuals, especially as the objective political and economic forces tend toward centralization. The trend toward collectivism is also strengthened by the psychic forces which have been neglected under the reign of reason and which demand satisfaction. The Marxist movement was definitely experienced as a freedom movement, and its basic anthropological thesis that "man is good" contains a kernel of truth: man's good tendencies do form part of his nature. Marxism may therefore be considered an attempt at self-healing in a society fragmented by individualism.

Because of its association with the materialist conception of history, however, Marxism immediately became an ethical vehicle for collectivism. The "leap from the realm of necessity into the realm of freedom" [4] was understood only in terms of man's technological liberation from nature, and the goal of

4. Engels, *loc. cit.*

social evolution was considered to be the liberation of the productive forces, i.e., the growth of productivity. Freedom thus came to be interpreted purely from the naturalistic point of view. Marxism did not aspire to ethical liberty but only to the freedom of instinctual man in his natural state—the freedom required for physical well-being. When it speaks of the subjection of the economic forces by man, it thinks only in terms of a system for the ownership and distribution of property. The Marxists not only welcomed the trend toward big business; they promoted it because they believed it to be necessary for the purpose of liberating man from the fetters of private property. Apart from this, Marxism required centralized planning, which made the "apparatus" even more powerful.

As a matter of fact, wherever Marxist principles have been put into effect, they have led to a tremendous inflation of the state rather than to its "withering-away." With liberation of the productive forces and increase of productivity as the highest goals for human action, man became ever more absolutely fettered by the apparatus. He had to sacrifice not only his emotional forces, his instincts, and his personal needs to the economy but also his personal freedom, because economic centralization is bound to lead to the establishment of authoritarian government. Further, it is obvious that a philosophy of life which conceives of human consciousness as a mere reflex of the conditions of production has no use for the moral dignity of the individual or for objective ethical values. The *raison d'état* is its sole ethical criterion, and man degenerates into a mere target for propaganda.

The scope of collective ethics is also limited by both the type of economy and the type of man involved. All ethical principles change once they are applied to reality. An absolute requisite becomes a relative postulate along with many others, since it has to adapt itself to the nature of the relevant field of application. The economy is of fundamental importance to man's survival, and it is therefore closely related to biological realities, which may be modified but can never be fundamentally changed by ethical standards. To a large extent, the economy has all the characteristics of an objective "shadow." In order to survive, it has to appeal to very strong motives, which, up to now, have been provided by the instinct of self-preservation (as in liberalism) and by fear or by force (as in communism). It is questionable whether a differentiated kind of motivation can ever be achieved unless man undergoes some inner transformation.

Furthermore, both economic and political phenomena are in fact mass phenomena. Those who are caught up in them cannot afford to show consideration for the personal situation of their partners without endangering their own existence or the objective goal. Both spheres are governed by well-defined patterns, and it is difficult to see how these might be changed, either as a result of a political approach to economics or by means of more centralization. In any event, individual morality can have only limited significance.

As the causal role played by the individuals involved in these processes can no longer be ascertained, it is also no longer possible to discern what is economically right and what is wrong. This is well illustrated by the example of the relative contribution made by individual groups of factory workers to the commercial success of a complete piece of equipment. In individual cases the imponderables play such an important role in influencing the end results that it becomes impossible to apply principles of justice. Consequently, the permanent aspects of the system have to be relied on more and more heavily, but this implies that "injustice" has to be accepted by all those involved. For purely objective reasons the ethical influence which can be exerted on mass phenomena is limited once they have been set in motion.

Many people have therefore come to the conclusion that only a change in the economic and social system can lead to ethical conduct in economics. In other words, only collective ethics can bring about justice. These same people say that we cannot expect any results from the personal transformation of the individual but that we can count on the moral evolution of man once he is educated by society and economic conditions have improved.

We feel that the economic system is, indeed, an eminently important instrument of government policy. It is of decisive importance for the economic and political destiny of a nation and therefore has to be carefully attended to. But it is not necessarily an instrument for the solution of ethical problems. All it can achieve is the safeguarding of a minimum of socioethical standards, given man's existing level of civilization and the blockage of his conscience. Apparently, instinctual man in his modern rational incarnation can put up with only a certain amount of inequality of wealth and power, because it is his nature to be abstract, egalitarian, and revolutionary. Even Montesquieu [5] pointed this out, when he said that commercialism created in man "un certain sentiment de justice exacte," which contrasts, on the one hand, with common plunder but is also incompatible with man's moral quality, preventing him from acting always in pure self-interest and obliging him to waive his own interests in favor of his fellow men. The effects of instinctual egalitarianism can be seen in people's reactions against authoritarian forms of government, monopoly control, and tax policies. From a purely abstract point of view it is indeed difficult to see why some people should have more money, more power, or more influence than others. Reality and experience alone can provide reasons for such discrimination; but reality and experience are becoming increasingly meaningless for modern man. While egalitarian ideas are only indirectly related to ethics, the ruling classes must take this mentality into account if they are not to risk the loss of power; their unawareness is related to rational man's inability to put himself in someone else's place. Another reason why careful attention must be paid to the economic system is that interplay of economic forces, like the interplay of other natural processes, is not necessarily harmonious. From time to time there

---

5. Montesquieu, *Esprit des lois*, ed. Destutt de Tracy et Villemain (Paris: Dalibon, 1827), Vol. II, Bk. XX, Chap. II, p. 264.

are dislocations and disturbances which need to be removed lest they become a pretext for revolutionary movements. As we said above, the rational world of modern civilization tends to repress man's emotional forces, which remain primitive and lend fuel to any latent opposition against the existing economic establishment and against reality in general.

Wisdom would undoubtedly counsel the ruling classes to fashion the economic system on the basis of social justice. Yet experience has clearly shown the dangers which mankind is likely to incur if it expects to solve all its problems by means of collective ethics or a change in the economic order. Justice, peace, and freedom from exploitation can be achieved only by means of personal ethical effort on the part of individuals.

The concepts of justice which are employed in the politicoeconomic struggle of our times were originally the offspring of our ethical ideals. In fact they are mere ideologies—in other words, political conveniences or rationalizations of interests rather than human values. Since moral accomplishments require spontaneous and creative activity, only individuals can become the carriers of ethical and spiritual progress. But this kind of specific ethical accomplishment presupposes inner independence of people and things. Values would have to be converted into facts, and man would have to feel free in his actions vis-à-vis the outside world of nature and society. This involves inner commitment, not striving after conformity. Ethics demands that social action should be only a means, never an end. Social institutions and organizations, such as the state, the economy, trade associations and unions, technology, and education, pursue only outer goals. They are amoral because they act in their own interest and thus out of a blind desire for self-preservation. Moral efforts must be made by human beings. Society can merely preserve ethical forces, and even in this it will succeed only to the extent that it caters to the emotional forces, which are the sole retainers of conscience in the form of ethical memory. Common people have moral traditions; this is less true of the educated classes, who merely promote ideologies and the formation of consciousness in the service of purpose. Our rational society, which also includes the modern state, does not promote ethical values in individuals (as Montesquieu pointed out) [6] but only conformism. It succeeds in transforming the instinct for self-preservation into aspiration for social importance, which, in spite of being apparently conformist, is a purely instinctual and egoistic attitude, like individualism itself.

No social order can create a community in the ethical sense of the word or bring about social harmony. Socialization of the means of production is no more a foundation for socialism than economic freedom is for liberalism. Once a certain optimum has been attained, guaranteeing man a dignified human existence, any extension of government power weakens individual responsibility. If a government were to attempt the elimination of all economic inequalities, it would have to interfere with the economy to such an extent as to render impossible the moral development of the individual. Moreover, we would be left with the same kind of bureaucracy that now exists in the economy. The individual has even less significance for the state than he has for the economy, because affairs of state are exclusively dominated by *raisons d'état*.

An increased influence of political economics and government, automatically entailing further centralization, would have the same effect. The influence of the individual—and thus of moral reflection and conscience—decreases as the power of collective interests increases, requiring a strengthening of central authority. Life becomes ever more mechanical, while local and regional initiative and particularities fade away. Natural cohesion is replaced by organized cohesion, and the form of government becomes increasingly dictatorial. Wherever it has not been possible to set up an authoritarian government, propaganda rather than ethical influence becomes the vehicle for achieving unity of purpose. This applies to the United States and Germany in particular, but even in Switzerland we can see the beginnings of this process. Ends justify the means, which is

6. *Ibid.*, p. 263.

only another way of saying that ethical values are sacrificed to the interests of the state. The individual is increasingly considered a nuisance and an enemy of the social system. He loses the ability to make ethical evaluations, and this inevitably leads to the loss of his conscience. Conscience is replaced by collective standards, considered to be the sole promoters of outer social goals. The personal integrity of the citizen is lowered as he becomes a stooge of propaganda.

We can easily demonstrate the truth of these assertions by means of a comparison between present-day small countries and the major powers. Switzerland has been able to preserve its emotional values, its national particularities, its original forms of social behavior, both in private life and in the public sector, to a much larger extent than the major powers. Its intellectual life is still much more governed by ethical considerations, and in economic life, as in private life, some of the instinctive features of behavior, lost in many of the bigger countries, have been preserved. Rational thinking and rational institutions are much less developed than elsewhere. At present, however, American influence has created an increasing tendency to look upon this national peculiarity as retrograde and to sacrifice it to the idols from abroad. This is brought out most clearly in attitudes toward current efforts on behalf of European union, which are strongly oriented toward economic and general centralization. Strangely enough, the tendency toward secularization is less apparent in economics and politics than in science. But this corresponds to the pattern according to which collectivization usually develops.

It has been shown how complete the cleavage has become between modern man's conscious and his unconscious, between his intellect and his instincts, between object-directed life and emotional life. It follows that the projection of his unconscious on other people and on his environment must be correspondingly great. In a world of collectivism and reason emotional values are considered bothersome. They are underrated and neglected, which means that, along with his conscience, modern man has also lost the ability to experience his inner wealth and spontaneity. This is why he expects to achieve progress— through improvement of his standard of living, education, technology—with outside help from the state, the economy, and the establishment in general. This is why he idealizes all these institutions and is left with the eschatological expectation that a reign of peace—of nonviolence and justice—will neces- sarily be brought about by means of an organizational scheme or new social system, i.e., by means of a new world order.

Apart from this kind of optimistic hope, the cleavage has also filled man with feelings of fear and impotence. Under the influence of collective ethics he has had to repress his instincts and emotional forces; but since they have not been cultivated, they continue to exist in the form of bad tendencies projected on other people, in whom they can be combated more success- fully. Frequently such a projection falls onto a social group or a partner who is in some way actually opposed to us. It may also be another country, another race, our own government, the police, the public treasury, or competitors, colleagues in our place of work, or our partner in marriage. In all these relationships we seem to look for the evil in other people, with the result that our repressed emotional forces give rise to complete distrust of all social relationships, depriving the frag- mented rational being of his ability to judge objectively or to identify with others. This is the reason for the inherent insolu- bility of East-West or employer-employee relations, as well as those between antagonistic branches of the economy or be- tween liberals and socialists. Another typical example is the insolubility of the problems of financial reform, which could be carried out only by means of a return to ethical standards now largely lost from consciousness.

Technology, government, the economy, science, and other sociocultural controls have become fatal to modern collective man only because of his inability to mobilize his ethical re- sources and to gain an objective view of the moral world. Since we have not succeeded in dealing with them ethically, these controls have converted themselves into autonomous forces which, because of their amorality, have become destructive.

At the same time, the degeneration of our ethical values has also been responsible for the generation of the very revolutionary forces which constantly jeopardize the rational structure of our culture. Yet the rational evolution of our cultural structure continues to make progress, with the result that the unconscious is incessantly fed new impulses which further strengthen the irrational "counterforces." In this way, it is believed, blind instinctual behavior or accident might eventually be ruled out. Actually they are reinforced through people's inability to realize that the causes of the conflict reside in their own unconscious. But the unconscious is most conservative by nature and is utterly unconcerned with political systems or rules governing the market-economy game. It could thus hardly be considered responsible for the lack of moral progress made by humanity in the last several thousand years.

THE REBIRTH OF CONSCIENCE

WITH THIS REALIZATION we can at least set a course which might lead to the retrieval of conscience. Inasmuch as conscience is embedded in man's emotional sphere, it can be developed only by enabling him to gain access to his blocked and neglected world of emotions. The royal road has been shown by C. G. Jung, and for the purpose of this paper we might simply conclude by pointing to his life's work. But the deeper meaning of this path can be understood properly only by one who has gone it a stretch of the way himself. For this reason the public at large, not to mention the world of economics, cannot have grasped the meaning of the fundamental changes in man's spiritual orientation which is brought about by the renuification of mind and nature and the resulting renewal of conscience. It might therefore be useful to describe some of the most important implications in terms of customary philosophical and religious concepts.

To begin with, such a change would imply that, in addition to outer reality—which for the naïve realist is the only one—we recognize inner reality as equally valid and real. Its timeless and "synchronistic" context is as real as naturalistic causal reality. Like Janus, consciousness would acquire two faces, enabling us to look at both worlds until we realized that they are in fact identical—that both are contained in the numinous reality of the Self and that we meet it in the polarity of the universal and the individual principles.

Psychologically, the unification of the two worlds may manifest itself in various ways: first, as union of the intellect and the instincts, or perhaps as that of the spiritual and the animal-vegetative world, providing man with a focus, which thinking, science, or ideology alone cannot afford him, as they do not involve the deeper layers of his psyche. He is thus enabled to replace abstract relationships with concrete roots in reality and is reunited with the forces of the psyche. On the basis of thousands of years of human experience these can orient him reliably in this world.

Elsewhere this process makes itself felt as union of ideals with reality, of light with shadow. Ideals do not spring from a vacuum. They must be acquired on the basis of human reality, which alone can bring them to life. Otherwise they remain in the realm of ideology derived from consciousness like almost all "ideas" which are applied in economics. In Jungian terms, for both employers and workers acceptance of their "own shadow" is the unconditional premise for the recovery of conscience. This is indispensable for the withdrawal of the projection of our destructive tendencies on other people and for the purpose of arriving at a creative as well as objectively thought-out solution of social problems. We might at least be able to make a beginning at mastering our instincts and at promoting a social development which would indeed lead from slavery to freedom. Finally, we might at last be in a position to achieve detachment from the collective forces, or—in psychological terms—to distinguish between personal action and mere intrusion of the archetypes.

A third aspect of the process shows itself in the concerted activity of the various psychic functions, i.e., thinking, feeling, sensation, and intuition, or the harmonization of hard realism with the world of emotion. Thinking is led back to its creative source, purifying and enlightening the other forces of the psyche and releasing them from their state of primitive undifferentiatedness. The ego loses its position of predominance, and man's actions are once more governed by the Self, by his creative and spontaneous center of activity. Emotion, the matrix of conscience and of human values in general, gains a place of respect and so can resist the overpowering pressures of outer purpose, which should actually be subservient to it. Once the individual is again in possession of a personal scale of values and no longer confuses the market value of things with their value for life, economic considerations begin to take their natural place in the over-all scale of values. Truly human relationships can take the place of abstract opportunist associations with our fellow men and with the state. Such is the revolutionary effect of inner transformation.

Neither knowledge nor education can provide us with the key to man's innermost being, his heart. It can be found only through an act of faith, a belief that the moral world will sustain us. We have to make a conscious decision that we are willing to face the risks involved in the polarity of grace and freedom. It means moving in a world whose axis is quite different from that of the outer world. Here, too, there is conformity with natural law, but it is individualized and varies according to the individual sphere assigned to each human being, the primordial image man has to measure up to if he is to reach his destination. Together with the concrete forces or abilities of his soul and environment this primordial image gives shape to human individuality. Every individual is related to others and to the cosmos by means of what psychology has designated as the archetypes. We might say that the psyche, and therefore conscience, has the specific task of acting as a link between divine destiny and self-determination, between the will of God and personal freedom, between the macrocosm and the microcosm, or whatever other names one may wish to give to these antinomian relationships. This is why everyone is duty-bound to determine the forces and conditions which constellate his life—his tendencies—so as to understand the *coniunctio rerum omnium*, the mysterious chain of providential circumstances which links all beings with their primordial element. To this end our dreams provide us with very important signposts.

Syntheses of all the above-mentioned contradictions can be achieved only with help from the world of images and symbols. Psychic reality seems to express itself exclusively in symbols for objective experiences, i.e., by means of persons (such as the "anima" or the "wise old man"), animals, plants, landscapes, the elements, or abstract configurations; it can never find final expression in words or concepts. These images are the regulating, anticipating, warning, punishing, and healing forces of our psyche as well as the spokesmen of our conscience.

We might say that images and symbols are the repositories of our psychic energy, making it accessible to us. The formation of will is apparently no more than the coming-to-life of these images. In the very nature of things these are autonomous, i.e., we have no more control over them than we have over the direction in which the wind is blowing. The only thing we can control are the dead remains, namely, concepts, though even they are not always at the disposal of our will. The living images can be grasped only through concentration; and, to the extent that we are able to focus our attention on them, we can control psychic energy. Yet even this possibility is subject to the antinomy of grace and freedom.

One aspect of this limitation upon our will should, however, console us. We are too easily inclined to view psychic activity from our own narrow perspective and to leave the solution of the world's problems to the individual efforts of the few people who seem to have achieved complete enlightenment or to those who are of the same opinion as we are. We tend to forget only too easily that our volition is dependent on the activity of the archetypes, which link our existence to the universal soul. In this context we might agree with Yitzchak Leib Perez, who said that unbelievers do not exist,[7] or we might agree that in fact all creatures "conspire to exalt Tao," [8] as Lao-tse put it, and that our own efforts are merely a part of something much bigger.

Since conscience belongs to the realm of these cosmic images, we must infer that a humanistic conscience, so-called, does not exist, as some psychoanalysts believe. Conscience might be more readily considered a gift or a curse of heaven, depending on how you look at it. All man can do is to exert his inner strength so as to make his conscience as clear and shining as possible and to contribute to its development.

On the other hand, conscience itself is a phenomenon beyond human consciousness, operating independently of man's willingness to respect it, consciously or not. There is therefore always a risk, in the eyes of some people, that it may seek to realize itself in ways that have a destructive effect on humanistic ideals or that it may seek spokesmen who belong to social classes or categories of population at present considered inferior. In this sense world history is also the Day of Judgment.

The correct attitude toward conscience is the same as the attitude we should have toward dreams. Both reveal their meaning through secret symbols. In order to unravel them, an act of courage and spontaneity is required which is often in paradoxical contradiction to the rational world of purposefulness. Here we are reminded of the paradoxes in the Sermon on the Mount, which have always been a hard nut to crack for both theologians and moralists and which can be understood only through similar personal experiences.

The Sermon on the Mount does not seem to contain moral commands, but it does provide man with guidance, enabling him to gain access to his inner world. In the language of modern psychology, we might say that it gives directives for a

---

7. Yitzchak Leib Perez, quoted by Felix Weltsch, *Gnade und Freiheit* (Munich: Kurt Wolff, 1920), p. 12.
8. Lao-Tse, Aphorism 51.

creative life. It focuses on the condition of neediness and poverty of mind which is the key to internal life and thus also to conscience. Such an attitude is anything but passive or, even worse, hypocritical. Quite on the contrary, it presupposes an act of tremendous spontaneity and spiritual independence. It frees us from the fetters of the collectivity and at the same time sets us apart from our fellow men. On the surface we become lonelier, although inwardly we feel much closer to people.

Like everything on the level of the psyche, this attitude has a thousand aspects and cannot be fully expressed in words. This is why I should like to try to formulate some of these aspects:

We always feel poor, unaware of the fact that plenty is within our reach, since we can partake of the inexhaustible riches of the unconscious.

We always feel helpless vis-à-vis life, but at the decisive moment we are imbued with a strength which is absent from purposeful consciousness.

We are forever insecure because we are confronted by the vicissitudes and the ultimate mystery of life, but in the end we proceed with the unerring safety of a sleepwalker.

Confronted with the infinity of the universe, we always feel inadequate; yet, looking back, we seem to have succeeded in all essential things, because we do not rely on the strength of the conscious but benefit from the help of the unconscious.

We are living in an alien world surrounded by strangers, but in the end we are rooted in our own soil, because we fully incorporate the alien into our being.

At the same time we can also see the other side of the coin.

We are not surprised to find that we no longer can go where we want but are led where we do not want to go.

We are fearful and yet always have to take on the most difficult tasks, because something new can spring only from an act of spontaneity.

We always live in fear of the unknown, and yet we find that it is our destiny to keep to the road, because the new can be conquered only by sacrificing the old.

We live in constant fear of the living God, who nonetheless enters through every crack of our house and every pore of our body.

We are constantly forced into situations, and yet we go from one free act to another, if we are ready to replace compulsion by ethical decision.

We are always behaving foolishly and making mistakes, but afterward we realize that in some mysterious way our mistakes turned out to be wise.

If we bear in mind this attitude, we come to the realization that conscience does not consist of a series of principles but of psychic forces which overcome us and which impart synthetic insight. Principles apply only to generalities and to past events, while decisions taken by conscience are unique and very personal. They are an act of creation which comes to life because it has been freely decided upon. It enters the realm of knowledge only after the event. Yet we must not surrender blindly to the call of conscience. On the contrary, it should enable us to take full advantage of the freedom within us.

We know now that in all essential decisions of conscience we also assume our share of guilt, whether we act or whether we refrain from acting. We are absolved from this guilt if we consciously assume full responsibility for our decisions. If, on the other hand, we shirk it, we risk falling prey to neuroses; for we sin if we do not act in faith. Only when it becomes necessary to make decisions of this kind do they become moral actions. All other decisions are determined by the law of nature.

This is undoubtedly the reason why our immoral actions are ethically effaced if we take them back by atonement for our desertion in the face of the spirit and in the exercise of our ethical freedom. Even repentance, we must realize, is not something that can be commanded. It is effective only if it also penetrates the unconscious. We can open ourselves to the unconscious, but we cannot control it. This is precisely why the attitude of neediness and meekness is so fundamentally important for our spiritual welfare.

Conscience, then, is the Word of God, which heals as well as wounds us. It is the razor's edge on which we encounter both grace and freedom.

The realists and the collectivists will ask: How does the world benefit from this attitude? Will it ensure social harmony, world peace, and freedom from exploitation, or at least the peace of mind promised by the various religious creeds? None of these goals can be reached directly. Direct solutions are only sham solutions, rationalist and ideological expedients, which do not at all touch man's innermost being and which are, therefore, easily made illusory by unconscious forces. Inner transformation is the sole road to the objectives man covets.

Even after this inner transformation has occurred, we continue to be faced with the same world. But we see it from inside ourselves and no longer just in its causal context. The context becomes meaningful, and we begin to understand it in the cosmic terms of values and the living forces of the soul. We begin to recognize that conscience is constantly at work to achieve human freedom, world peace, and justice. Its collaborators are, however, few and far between, as most people are given over to the hopeless task of dominating, improving, and educating others or of surrounding themselves with a rational shell designed to protect themselves against the clutches of the living God. Unless the instincts are controlled, all individual or collective efforts to bring about peace and justice will be condemned to failure. This is why inner transformation is an unconditional prerequisite for both.

Even if we are ready to submit to this process of inner metamorphosis, we still come up against ourselves with all our good and bad characteristics; but we shall place them at the service of our own and other people's inner transformation. We shall be able to accept our good traits as mere gifts of heaven, not entitling us to any special merit, while our negative traits must be recognized as inevitable shadows which we must endure if we want to stay on this side of reality.

Our personal or social partners and opponents will still be with us, but they will become our educators and collaborators. In other words, we shall continue to play the same social role, but in the knowledge that we may not take credit for it. We shall realize that it is the work of that mysterious power called accident, which fills us with justified fear, though perhaps not enough of it, if we build up rational fences around it. We shall even assume the responsibility for our adversaries to the extent that we accept them as part of our unconscious. This places all of us on an equal footing, provided we do not believe that we can determine other people's destiny by rational means; for we cannot be responsible for the whole world.

We shall still have to face all the cruelty of this world, but in awareness of the fact that unconsciously we all have a major share in causing it. As Heraclitus put it, "Every beast is driven to pasture with blows," [9] or, as in the Old Testament formulation, God makes peace and creates evil.[10] For this reason we should reverse the question about the cause of all evil; like J. G. Hamann, we might be astonished to find that "finite creatures are capable of being good and happy." [11]

This new attitude does not give us any guarantee that we shall be spared the adversities of life on either the individual or the collective level. Whosoever has had occasion to look into the depths of his unconscious is much more astonished to find that the world is not worse off than it is. Yet, even if the worst should happen to us, even if we should be unable to withstand "brain-washing," we shall at least have the certainty that we

9. [Frag. 55, trans. John Burnet, *Early Greek Philosophy*, 4th ed. (London: Adam & Charles Black, 1945), p. 137. Cf. Philip Wheelwright, *Heraclitus* (Princeton: Princeton University Press, 1959), Chap. III and Appendix B, "Notes on the Fragments," p. 143. Burnet and Bywater-Loeb Frag. 55 = Wheelwright Frag. 41 = Diels-Kranz Frag. 11.—EDITOR.]

10. [Isaiah 45:7: "I [the Lord] make peace and create evil" (AV).—TRANSLATOR.]

11. Johann Georg Hamann, *Sämtliche Werke* (Vienna: Thomas Morus Presse, 1949), I, 305.

have gained a firm ground on which to stand by having attained to the highest values, i.e., the fullness of our psychic life.

Finally, we shall again be confronted by our good as well as our bad conscience. How could it be otherwise? If we had only a good conscience, we should be fully identifying with the spirit of our times, i.e., with only one extreme of reality, while we should have to live in constant fear of the other one, which we are so strenuously trying to ignore. We should, therefore, be unfit for work in the Kingdom of Heaven, except as God's scourge, which has been from time immemorial one of the most sought-after professions of "righteous" men in economics as well as in the affairs of the state and the church. We should, therefore, be glad that this profession, too, was created by God.

Even fear will not disappear, since it is a fundamental phenomenon. We might overcome it in some isolated instances to the extent that we succeed in accepting the refuse of the constant process of transformation, to which even our deepest insights and best deeds are subject. We shall also have to refrain from carrying our acquisitive spirit over into the realm of the soul by making God our private property. We should only succeed in giving free play to the Devil outside our rational human fences, which, it is to be feared, he would be able to topple with the greatest of ease. The more frankly we can face the contents of our conscience, the more easily we shall be able to deal with our fears. But the more we try to erect safety barriers to protect ourselves, the more we try to fence ourselves in, the more terrible will be the experience of the living God.

Inflation of evil can be avoided if we realize that light and shadow, ideal and reality, mind and matter, reason and unreason, good and bad conscience, are unalterable facts of psychic reality. It follows that we are equally unable to overcome the antagonism between employers and employees, socialists and liberals, East and West, and that we can only submit it to our conscience. On the other hand, we often tend not to take this antagonism seriously enough. We obscure it by means of ideologies instead of coping with it inside ourselves. For the same reason, we cannot escape the shadow-side of the economy as a biological reality without running the risk of becoming unrealistic and utopian.

The union of all opposites is a never-ending task, for new pairs of opposites are constantly generated by the continuing life process. Opposites are, however, the standards for all our actions, and we must take them into consideration. Otherwise we would risk losing our sense of proportion. We might even become victims of one or the other extreme, thinking that it would help us to overcome the contradictions. If we try to do away with opposites, we have to pay for the resulting hybrid with the fragmentation of the individual and society. The cruel effects of this experiment can be felt at present. As idealists we despise reality, and as realists we despise the spirit; the result is that we have become conscienceless in both realms.

The alliance of knowledge and conscience does not imply that they would ever become one in reality—except in action. It does imply that man would continually try to bring them into living contact with each other. Man is not a standard, but with the help of symbols he may become the focal point of the opposites, coming closer to wholeness by means of inner transformation.

Meeting a fellow student on the road, the monk Tao-Chien, who for many years had been trying to penetrate the mysteries of Zen, once had an experience, which also applies to inner transformation. He was told:

> . . . there are some things in which I cannot be of any help to you; these you must look after for yourself. . . . For instance, when you are hungry or thirsty, my eating of food or drinking will not fill your stomach; you must eat and drink for yourself. When you want to respond to the calls of nature, you must take care of yourself, for I cannot be of any use to you. And then it will be nobody else but yourself that will carry your body along this highway.[12]

12. D. T. Suzuki, *An Introduction to Zen Buddhism*, ed. Christmas Humphreys (London: Rider & Co., 1948), p. 90.

Angelus Silesius expressed the same idea in Christian terms: "Even if Christ is born a thousand times at Bethlehem, unless He is born in you, you will be lost everlastingly." [13] Realization of the import of this aphorism will release a personal religious experience and may provide us with a hint concerning the true meaning of conscience.

13. Angelus Silesius, *Des Angelus Silesius Cherubinischer Wandersmann*, ed. Wilhelm Bölsche (Jena, 1914), p. 63.

The Concept of Conscience in Jewish Perspective

R. J. Zwi Werblowsky

Translated by R. F. C. Hull

Anyone who asks himself what might be the meaning and validity of a certain concept within a particular culture will do well to try translating it into the language of that culture. Very often he will find it changing under his hand into something else, not least because words, like all symbols, acquire their proper meaning only from their structural and functional associations. Even more instructive is the occasional discovery of the sheer untranslatability of concepts from one language into another. The complete failure to find even an approximate rendering replaces the original question regarding the meaning and validity of the concept by a new one: does an equivalent of what is denoted by our concept exist at all in the culture we are examining?

To let the cat out of the bag at once: there is no Hebrew equivalent of our Western "conscience"—not even an approximation. This is all the more remarkable because, in the Hellenistic period and then again in the Middle Ages, under the influence of Arabic philosophy, Rabbinic Hebrew absorbed a large number of concepts that originally were alien to it. Yet conscience was not one of them.[1] If by a "concept of con-

---

Discrepancies between this translation and the original German text are due to revisions made by the author in English.—TRANSLATOR.

1. The modern Hebrew *mazpun* (*infra*, p. 90) is a neologism or, rather, a late modification of the meaning of an older word with a different content.

science in Jewish perspective" we mean a doctrine of conscience derived from Jewish sources, we are presenting ourselves with a nonexistent theme, for which, by definition, no
sources exist. Nothing characterizes this awkward situation
more plainly than the apologetic attempts of well-meaning
Jewish writers to prove that Judaism is no whit inferior to
other Western religious and ethical systems and that it attributes to conscience a fundamental significance. Thus (to cite
only one example) we have it on authority [2] that conscience is
"an essential element in Jewish ethics"; but this assertion is
supported by nothing except an enumeration of virtues whose
religious and ethical value is determined by their *contents*
(love, charity, holiness, imitation of God, and so on) and not
by any formal properties. I do not wish to deny that the
material contents of Jewish religious ethics agree at many
points with those of an ethic of conscience, yet this agreement
is no proof of the central importance, let alone the existence, of
conscience in the system of Jewish morality.

Awkward though this state of affairs is, it is not lacking in
irony. It would be altogether too strange if the very people
who, according to the unanimous testimony of all enemies of
the Biblical-Jewish-Christian world of values, are to be
"blamed" for depriving civilized man of his elemental affirmation of life and for "afflicting" him with a conscience should
themselves be "conscience-less" in the most literal sense of the
word!

There remains, then, only the more uncomfortable, indirect
approach to our problem, via two introductory questions. First
of all, what do *we* mean when we say "conscience"? And
second, to what anthropological structure, to what aspect of
human existence, does this concept correspond, so that, start-
ing from there, we could try to lay hold of its possible coun-
terpart in the Jew? Is conscience something characteristic of

2. *Encyclopedia of Religion and Ethics,* ed. James Hastings (Edin-
burgh, 1908–27), *s.v.* "Conscience, Jewish."

particular cultures, or does it represent a general human structure whose form alone varies?

Our first task, therefore, is to describe what conscience is,
not to "explain" it. Even if, as children of the twentieth
century, we cannot help thinking in psychogenic terms, we
are nevertheless dealing here with a fundamental anthropological fact transcending all empirical psychology. However much
of the unconscious we project into an objective world of
values, or, conversely, however much we introject parental
imagos as inner imperatives, the basic anthropological problem
remains the same: how are we able to do the one or the other?
For our present purpose, however, the essential ground structure of our human mode of being is more fundamental than the
mechanisms through which it expresses itself.

The word "conscience" appears in our linguistic usage as a
translation of the classical terms *syneidēsis, conscientia.*[3] It is
primarily a "knowing-with"; but the person with whom (or
thing with which) man knows (*syneidēnai tini ti; scire aliquid
cum aliquo*) is his own self (*syneidēnai heautōi ti*). Poets as
well as philosophers made use of this expression, but it was
only with the Stoics that it acquired an ethical nuance, probably for the simple reason that knowledge of—or being conscious of—the structure (*systasis*) of the cosmos determines
ethical behavior, which is nothing other than being in harmony with the cosmos. In Cicero the ethical undertone is
clearly perceptible, and in the New Testament[4] *syneidēsis*
appears less as conscience in the sense of an evaluation of
particular actions than as a consciousness coterminous with the
conduct of life as a whole, so that one is inclined to equate
Paul's concept of *syneidēsis* with the spirit (*ruah*) of holiness,
or else of impurity and sin, indwelling in man. As the voice
that accompanies and judges every action, it is the embodiment

3. Cf. Gertrud Jung, "Syneidēsis, Conscientia, Bewusstsein," *Archiv
für die gesamte Psychologie,* LXXXIX (1933), 525 ff.
4. This subject is touched on only in passing, as it is discussed more
fully by more competent authorities elsewhere in this symposium.

of the divine core in man, also known as *synterēsis;* and there may well be a direct line linking the *scintilla conscientiae* of Saint Jerome with Meister Eckhart's "little spark."

Nevertheless, the Schoolmen were far from making conscience an autonomous authority that creates values. They conceived of its function rather as reflecting, or reacting to, an existing reality; according to Saint Bonaventure, conscience is *sicut praeco Dei et nuntius* ("like a herald and messenger of God"). As with most problems in the Middle Ages, it was Thomas Aquinas who synthesized the many aspects of conscience in a valid formula: "For conscience is said to witness, to bind or incite, and also to accuse, sting, or rebuke." [5] Here we have conscience complete, as we know it. Only its autonomy and its individual creative power are denied: "Man does not make up a law for himself; but by his act of recognizing the law made [for him] by another, he binds himself to its observance." [6] Perhaps we may summarize the teachings of the "angelic doctor" as follows: reason cognizes, but conscience recognizes and acknowledges the binding, obligatory force (*ligatur*) of what is cognized by reason. His doctrine, based on Greek rationalism no less than on revealed religion, may be a first indication of the necessity of conscience for the man who wants to live, not out of himself, but in relation to an order *ab alio factam.*

It is not, however, the moral content of conscience that appears to be the really fundamental and, from the anthropological standpoint, the decisive thing. It is rather, as the word itself implies, the psychological fact of "knowing-with," *conscientia* as "con-scious-ness" (as the term was used after Descartes), which is our main concern. To put it even more precisely: it is not so much consciousness as consciousness of

5. "Dicitur enim conscientia testificari, ligare vel instigare, vel etiam accusare, vel etiam remordere sive reprehendere," *Summa Theologica,* I. 79. 13.

6. "Homo non facit sibi legem; sed per actum suae cognitionis qua legem ab alio factam cognoscit, ligatur ad legem implendam," *De Veritate,* 3, ad 1.

oneself that is the hub about which everything turns. This being given to oneself as both subject and object has been termed by Plessner the "positionality of ex-centric form" [7] and is described by him as the form of existence typical of man. Whatever man knows or experiences, it is always "with." As a result, his naturalness and "immediacy" are gone forever. Expelled from the paradise of "centric positionality," he is condemned—or shall we say exalted?—to a "mediate" form of existence. A psychologist puts it this way: "Having consciousness means having immediate experience of something mediate —it is the linguistic objectivation of one's own state. . . . When you say, 'Man is a being endowed with consciousness,' it means that his life includes the mediate within its immediacy." [8] If we call this mediate form of existence the dimension of the spirit, we shall have to agree with Nietzsche when he says: "Spirit is the life that itself cuts into life." [9] The only consolation for man, this thinking reed, who knows *of* himself and *with* himself, is the knowledge that precisely because of his divided state he is "superior to himself and the world" (Max Scheler).

But the nature of this ex-centric positionality is not limited to knowledge. It is also action or, to be more exact, having to act. Were he not imprisoned in his own dichotomy and duality, simultaneously inside and outside himself, "this side and that side of the gulf, bound in the body, bound in the psyche, and at the same time nowhere," [10] he might perhaps—like the God of Aristotle, who reposes in himself thinking himself—be an exponent of pure ex-centricity.[11] But man is not like God— not even like the God of Aristotle. The ex-centric structure not only "is"; it is continually "becoming." It compels man continually to rise above himself and the world. Man lives a

7. *Die Stufen des Organischen und der Mensch,* 2d ed. (Berlin, 1965).
8. P. R. Hofstätter, *Einführung in die Tiefenpsychologie* (Vienna, 1948), p. 37.
9. [*Thus Spake Zarathustra,* Part Two, "Of the Famous Philosophers."—TRANSLATOR.]
10. Plessner, *op. cit.,* p. 291.
11. Cf. F. Sierksma, *De religieuze projectie* (Delft, 1956), pp. 76 ff.

"human" life only when he is constantly "creating" it.[12] Hence the practically unanimous agreement of all thinkers with an anthropological turn of mind as to the paradoxically dualistic nature of man as a being that has to create or realize itself. "L'homme est ce qu'il n'est pas, et il n'est pas ce qu'il est" (Sartre). To be a human being means to become, to exist in time, to act, to act in freedom; and this, if you like, is the ethical aspect of *conscientia* or the French *conscience*, which splits into *consciousness* and *conscience* in English and *Bewusstsein* and *Gewissen* in German.

> Conscience gives me detachment from myself. I am not subjected to myself as to a being-in-the-world that is "given" and merely enacted. I act upon myself, and out of my being-in-the-world produce what I am, so far as lies within my power. Between my being-in-the-world and my being authentically myself, not yet revealed to me, is interposed the reality of conscience, through which I must acknowledge or reject what for me should become being.[13]

Thus our concern is with the man who comes "to himself," who seeks in bondage to himself and in detachment from himself to realize his freedom. The question of a Jewish view of conscience, since it cannot be posed directly, reduces itself to (or broadens into) the existential question of the "being" of the Jew in general. What does he know of? And *with* what? Wherein consists the freedom of the "conscience-less" Jew to intervene in his own being, shackled as he is in his "bondage to the Law"? [14]

II

LET US BEGIN with the biblical Jew. He, too, knows of a specifically human mode of existence,[15] and it is precisely this, with its implicit capacity for objectivation, that makes him

---

12. *Ibid.*, p. 26.
13. Karl Jaspers, *Philosophie* (Berlin, 1932), II, 268.
14. To cite once again the caricature of Judaism customary in theological literature.
15. ". . . in the image of God" (Gen. 1:27).

lord of creation.[16] Yet the created world is not his only object; he is no less an object to himself. As soon as he "finds" himself, in this case in the Garden of Eden,[17] he experiences in his own being a command, telling him "what for him should become being." According to the Bible story, to *be* is to *be addressed:* without freedom, as in Creation at large ("And God said . . . and it was so"),[18] or in freedom, as on the specifically human level ("And the Lord commanded the man, saying . . .").[19] God's ontological "saying" turns, in man's *conscientia*, into a "command." The response comes only from him who hears the command, who is "ob-edient" (Lat. *ob + audire*, "to hear"). Obedience to God's word and command means, for the biblical man, his own self-realization: "God . . . said unto him, Abraham: and he said, Behold, here I am." [20] Disobedience means not responding, evading respons-ibility, shutting oneself off from one's true being. The unanswered command becomes a reproach, conscience becomes a bad conscience: "And they heard the voice of the Lord walking in the garden in the cool of the day, and Adam and his wife hid themselves. . . . And the Lord God called unto Adam, and said unto him, Where art thou?" [21]

Not many words are needed to make clear how completely the fundamental human situation is experienced here in the form of a radical personal projection. God knows, sees into the heart, tries the heart and reins. The realization of man's being consists in a dialectical relationship, in going along with God, in a strong personal bond grounded in obedient response. The idea of the "covenant" thus became one of the pillars of biblical theology. This idea and the prophetic preaching of the divine commands, together with the rabbinic doctrine of the Law, once more affirm the validity of the phenomenological difference between the mystical and the prophetic type of

16. ". . . have dominion over the fish of the sea," etc. (Gen. 1:26, 28).
17. Gen. 2:15.
18. Gen. 1:9.
19. Gen. 1:16.
20. Gen. 22:1.
21. Gen. 3:8–9.

religion. Whereas mysticism, if radical enough, ultimately aims at overcoming dualism and thus abolishing conscience, the prophetic type of religion strives for its acceptance and constant reaffirmation.

We must, nevertheless, try to bring the situation we have just sketched into clearer focus. *Who* is the man whose conscience has knowledge of the voice of God (as revealed for instance in the Law)? To *whom* is this voice and its command addressed? First of all, quite simply and concretely, to the man who thinks, feels, desires; who—just because he is human—knows that he thinks, feels, desires, and what he ought to do. Man as an individual thus has an "inward part," though certainly no "soul" as yet; the description of the inward part as a soul is the product of a later development. The totality of man discloses itself in a variety of aspects, and for each of these aspects or modes of behavior there is in Hebrew a concrete expression corresponding to it: "foot" for movement, "hand" for action, "heart," "reins," or "bowels" for the whole of man's inner life. The heart is not only the physiological center; it is also the seat of the affections, of knowledge and desire, as well as of moral sentiment. In biblical language the heart is "upright," "stubborn," "hard," "crooked," etc. The reins (kidneys) have a similar function. God, who sees into or knows the inward parts, "tries the reins and the heart," [22] and, when he addresses man, he addresses the reins and heart also, not merely the hand and foot. But this voice is not the voice *of* the inward parts, rather it is addressed *to* them! We should not gloss over the difference between the biblical man and the modern man convinced of the moral dignity of the autonomous conscience. Truth does not come *out of* the heart, though it should enter *into* the heart: "And these words, which I command thee this day, shall be [written] in thine heart." [23] Thus the author of Deuteronomy. The prophets, having had bitter experience of the hardness and obduracy of the heart, lacked the optimism of

22. Jer. 11:20.
23. Deut. 6:6.

the Deuteronomist's injunction. God's word is not so easily engraved upon the human heart, and in their despair the prophets saw no other solution than the gift of a new heart created by God. But neither is this new heart of flesh, in place of the old, stony heart, a metaphor for the divine voice coming from within. No, the prophetic hope for the future affirms only that the word of God will in the end penetrate into man's heart and remain written there. That it has not done so yet is less the fault of God's Law than of man's obduracy.

> For this commandment which I command thee this day, it is not hidden from thee, neither is it far off. It is not in heaven, that thou shouldst say, Who shall go up for us to heaven, and bring it unto us, that we may hear it, and do it? Neither is it beyond the sea. . . . But the word is very nigh unto thee, in thy mouth, and in thy heart, that thou mayest do it.[24]

Man and God's Law (Torah) are not incompatible. On the contrary, they are related and attuned to each other. The notion of a "pre-established harmony" between man and the Torah which is implicit in this last quotation from Deuteronomy could be formulated thus: the Torah is man-like and man is Torah-like.[25] Knowledge, including conscience, is the affair of the inner man or heart. How closely the concepts "inward," "secret," "knowledge" are interfused is apparent from Ecclesiastes 10:22,[25a] where the word *madda*, "knowledge," simply means the secret inner part. The Torah may be of transcendental origin, but the response to it has to come from man's "inward parts."

No doubt the inward parts also include moral consciousness and the judging conscience, the "agenbite of inwit." When David cut off the skirt of Saul's robe, "it came to pass afterward that David's heart smote him,"[26] the Hebrew word *leb*,

---

24. Deut. 30:11–14.
25. I owe this formulation (based on a well-known poem by Goethe) to the late Isaac Breuer.
25a. If we keep to the Masoretic text. [AV has "Curse not the king, no not in thy thought."—TRANSLATOR.]
26. I Sam. 24:6.

"heart," standing here, as is usual in the Old Testament, for our "conscience." This use of the word is not unknown also in the non-Hebrew literature of the ancient Near East, and even the apocryphal books of the Old Testament, which show a fairly strong Hellenistic influence, use the same image.[27] I know of only one passage where the Greek term replaces the Hebrew *leb*. In the Testaments of the Twelve Patriarchs the dying Reuben warns his children against sin and, mindful of his own transgression, confesses "until now my conscience [*hē syneidēsis mou*] has tormented me."[28] Yet, as I have said, it remains characteristic of Jewish literature that the concept of *conscientia* did not gain currency and was therefore not translated. The Talmudic language of the rabbis, who were quite familiar with pangs of conscience and scruples, still speaks only of the "beating" or "palpitating" heart,[29] and even Bahya ibn Pakuda (Spain, eleventh century), one of the most outstanding representatives of the ascetic spirituality that blossomed under the influence of Neoplatonism and Sufism, calls his beautiful and widely read work "The Book of the Duties of the Heart." Here again the heart means the whole inner man, so it is quite understandable that Bahya should call his science of the spiritual life also the science of the heart, of the soul, or of the world within, making no distinction between these terms. In view of our interpretation of moral conscience as one aspect of *conscientia* in general, and hence as a differentiated manifestation of the inner world duplicated in the "ex-centric," mediate form of existence, the history of the word chosen by the Hebrew translator of Bahya's Arabic original is instructive. For it is no accident that this same word for the "inward" or, more accurately, "hidden" (*mazpun*) part of man later took on the connotation of "conscience" in the narrower, moral sense.

Man's capacity for projecting the entire ex-centric structure

27. Testament of Judah (in the Testaments of the Twelve Patriarchs) 20:5; Testament of Gad 5:3.
28. Testament of Reuben 4:3.
29. For instance, the rabbinic phrase *mi schelibbo nokefo*, "he whose heart palpitates."

has already been mentioned. When, however, it is not ex-centricity as a formal structure that is projected, but the ex-centric center itself, it presents itself to man as an experience of God. From the standpoint of psychic equilibrium [30] this means that man, by objectifying himself, confronts his own transcendent center, while at the same time experiencing himself as the continual object of this center, which can never be caught up with, never transcended, never captured. Plessner formulates it thus:

> Man "has" himself, knows of himself, is perceptible to himself, and by virtue of this he is an "ego," the vanishing point of his own inwardness. He is always "behind" himself, as it were, beyond any possibility of living directly out of his own center of being. In this sense he is beyond objectivation, a pole of subjectivity that cannot be put in the position of an object; a *spectator* watching the scenario of his own interior life.[31]

This quotation is apposite here because the projection of the "watching spectator" is expressed with unsurpassable clarity as an experience of God [32] in Psalm 139:

> O Lord, thou hast searched me, and known me.
> Thou knowest my downsitting and mine uprising,
>   thou understandest my thought afar off.
> Thou compassest my path and my lying down,
>   and art acquainted with all my ways.
> For there is not a word in my tongue,
>   but lo, O Lord, thou knowest it altogether.
> Thou hast beset me behind and before,
>   and laid thine hand upon me.
> Such knowledge is too wonderful for me;
>   it is high, I cannot attain unto it.
> Whither shall I go from thy spirit?
>   Or whither shall I flee from thy presence?
> If I ascend into heaven, thou art there,
>   if I make my bed in hell, behold, thou art there.

30. Cf. Sierksma, *op. cit.*, esp. pp. 55 ff.
31. Plessner, *op. cit.*, p. 290. My italics.
32. The theologian will say: an experience of God corresponding to the structure of human ex-centricity.

If I take the wings of the morning,
  and dwell in the uttermost parts of the sea,
Even there shall thy hand lead me,
  and thy right hand shall hold me.
If I say, Surely the darkness shall cover me,
  even the night shall be light about me;
Yea, the darkness hideth not from thee,
  but the night shineth as the day.

. . . .

Search me, O God, and know my heart,
  try me, and know my thoughts;
And see if there be any wicked way in me,
  and lead me in the way everlasting.[33]

Conscience is not always experienced in such radical projection. The biblical man too, like the theologian of a later day, could not but experience conscience—be it the guiding, the admonitory, or the "pricking" conscience—inwardly and, as it were, "introjected." This does not mean that he went to the other extreme and, taking back his projection in the modern fashion, ever thought of his conscience as an autonomous, immanent authority, let alone that he ever formulated the paradox of the human situation in psychological terms by asserting that "transcendence encounters man from his own psychic background." [34] The traditional religious attitude is content with the formula (or compromise?) that the inner voice is indeed the voice of God,[35] which, instead of passing through the tympanum and other organs of perception, resounds within him as conscience. That God's voice and this "within" can coincide or interpenetrate is evident from Psalm 16:7: "I will bless the Lord, who hath given me counsel: my reins also instruct me in the night seasons." [36] The characteristic

33. Verses 1–12, 23–24.
34. The unsurpassable formula by Rivkah Schärf, "Die Gestalt des Satans im Alten Testament," in C. G. Jung, *Symbolik des Geistes* (1948), p. 155, n. 4. [See the American edition of this work, Rivkah Schärf Kluger, *Satan in the Old Testament*, trans. Hildegard Nagel, Studies in Jungian Thought (Evanston, Ill., 1967), p. 5.—EDITOR.]
35. *Supra*, pp. 83–84.
36. The usual, less literal translation is "in the night also my heart instructs me," as in RSV.

parallelism between the two halves of a verse in Hebrew poetry, particularly marked in the Psalms, leaves us in no doubt that the "reins" (it could just as well have been "heart") correspond exactly to the voice of God. Even though the main point here is counsel and instruction, it is easy to see how the "instruction and admonition of the reins" later acquired the specific meaning of "pangs of conscience."

III

SINCE THE TIME OF HELLENISM, theologians have regarded the soul as the vessel of divine knowledge within man. In Proverbs 20:27, the soul [37] is called "the candle of the Lord, searching all the inward parts of the belly." Here the above-mentioned "watching" and all-knowing capacity of the soul is considered to be its true function. Rashi, the most important of the rabbinic commentators of the Middle Ages (eleventh century), accordingly explains this verse by giving it an eschatological and moralizing twist: "The soul indwelling in man will testify against him at the judgment." Another commentator [38] says the same thing even more plainly: "Even as a man searches in the darkness by means of a light, God searches out the innermost thoughts of a man by means of the soul, for it knows everything and will testify against him at the judgment."

We recall here the first function of conscience as defined by Thomas Aquinas: "Conscience is said to witness." Yet if the soul is a permanent witness or, in Plessner's words, a "spectator watching the scenario of the interior life," the question arises with renewed force: *Who* exactly is the essential, actual man that is being watched? He cannot be identified with the soul any more than he can with reason—the less so as any such differentiation of the functions or faculties was unknown in

---

37. The translation "soul" is proposed with reserve. In my view the passage refers to the soul in the later sense of a "soul substance" and not to the "breath of life." [In AV and RSV it is "spirit."—TRANSLATOR.]
38. Mezudath David.

the terminology of the ancient rabbis. The inward parts, whether heart or reins, naturally contain feeling, thinking, understanding, but it is the integral man who is in himself ex-centric and paradoxical. No doubt the ex-centric man is a being "superior to himself and the world," [39] but we must not expect rabbinic literature to provide a systematic anthropology that plumbs the essence of this being. On the other hand, partial aspects and certain concrete problems relevant to our theme are discussed at length, though not always consistently, in a figurative language hovering between myth and allegory.

The heart is mentioned often enough in the Talmud and the midrashim. The function of the brain being still unknown to rabbinic physiology, the heart remained for a long time the organ of thinking and understanding. As the inward part that instructs man,[40] it comes very close to reason. According to the rabbis, the patriarch Abraham broke away from the pagan world around him on his own initiative and arrived by himself at a knowledge of God. He was, so to speak, the inventor of natural theology! The rabbis, who had their own particular style of fabulation, credited the patriarchs not only with a theoretical knowledge of the existence of the Creator but also with a scrupulous observance of all the precepts of the written and oral law. "The Torah was not given to them, yet they followed it of their own accord." [41] Probably two different tendencies worked together to produce this view. First, the desire on the part of the ancient rabbis to present the patriarchs, even though they lived before the revelation of the Law on Sinai, as the type of perfect Jew, and then—and this was perhaps even more important—a rationalism of Greek prove-

39. *Supra*, p. 85. Thomas Aquinas shows very nicely how the problem of being superior to oneself can be dealt with in theological-philosophical projection: "Although man is not superior to himself, yet he of whose command he has knowledge is superior to him and hence he can be said to be bound by his conscience" (*Summa Theol.*, *loc. cit.*).

40. A midrash relates that for Abraham his two kidneys were "like two teachers."

41. Cf. *Mishnah*, Kiddushin 4:14 and Albeck's note *ad loc.* (Chanoch Albeck, *Commentary on the Mishnah* [Jerusalem, 1955], III, 416).

nance. This rationalism, absorbed into Judaism, maintained that revelation was not so much an expression of God's will or love as of his wisdom. The Torah, Sophia, and Logos were equated with one another. The problem that finally resulted from this: "Why, then, a revelation at all?" was to occupy the theologians and philosophers of the Middle Ages for a long time to come. Yet in contrast to the development that led from the wisdom literature of the Bible through Hellenistic thinking to medieval religious philosophy, popular Judaism, instinct with the life and warmth of religion, was little influenced by this rationalistic view of the Torah. The Torah is the revelation of God's will and of his law. The "inward part" of man is of significance only insofar as it too is addressed by God's law but is less easily brought to obedience than the body. Hence the aim of the "conscientious" Jew was to make the Torah, so far as possible, an inward possession. In further developing the theme already suggested in Deuteronomy,[42] the rabbis anticipated the notion of the introjection of conscience by nearly two thousand years. With reference to a rather artificially construed contradiction in Psalm 1:2, where it is said of the righteous man that "his delight is in the law of the Lord, and in his [43] law doth he meditate day and night," the Talmud observes that what, for the righteous man, was still God's law at the beginning of his development will in the end have become his own law. The heart, therefore, must make the Torah its possession. But human ex-centricity is infinite, and hence it is well-nigh impossible to possess the whole heart, as the prophet Jeremiah well knew when he lamented, "The heart is deceitful above all things, and desperately wicked: who can know it?" [44] The Greek translator was not so far from the truth when he rendered the opening words as "the heart is unfathomable." But man tries to confront his unfathomable and deceitful nature, grounded as it is in his ex-centric positionality, and he

42. *Supra*, p. 88.
43. Construed as referring not to the law of the Lord but to the righteous man's own law!
44. Jer. 17:9.

does so primarily by means of projection. Jeremiah continues: "I the Lord search the heart, I try the reins." [45] It is precisely with regard to the secret thoughts, known only to the heart, so the Talmud says,[46] that the Bible repeatedly admonishes us to "fear God." For "God requires the heart, as is said,[47] 'but the Lord looketh on the heart.' " [48] Tempests and other cataclysms of nature, overwhelming in their magnificence, "were created to make straight the crooked ways of the heart," [49] and certain sacrifices were intended to "atone for the thoughts of the heart." [50] Indeed, the heart, that is to say, the whole inner man, is created only "to speak the truth, as is said,[51] 'and he speaketh the truth in his heart.' " [52]

The problem of man's wholeness and truthfulness brings us to the most important and influential doctrine of rabbinic psychology, which shaped the traditional Jewish moral consciousness for many generations to come: the doctrine of the good and the evil inclination (*yeser*). "Two inclinations did the Holy One, Blessed be He, create; the one is the good inclination, the other the evil inclination." [53] The inner man is nothing but the battleground of these two inclinations. Man himself, round whom the battle rages, is not defined conceptually in this anthropology, except that in some texts the good inclination recedes into the background, so that the dialectic is played out between man and his evil inclination: "The evil inclination is like a fly, sitting between the two chambers of the heart." [54] It is only when man is viewed in the light of concepts originating in other spheres of thought that the good inclination, for instance, is identified with the heavenly soul. The commandment: "Thou shalt love the Lord thy God with

45. Jer. 17:10.
46. B. Kiddushin 32b.
47. B. Sanhedrin 106b.
48. I Sam. 16:7.
49. B. Berakoth 59a.
50. Lev. Rabbah VII.
51. Aboth de R. Nathan 58.
52. Psalm 15:2.
53. B. Berakoth 61a.
54. *Ibid.*

all thine heart" [55] is interpreted as "with both thine inclinations," [56] for the heart pulls us in two directions. "The heart and the eyes [57] are the pimps of sin," [58] or "the pimps of the body which commits the sin." [59] The good and the evil inclination are also represented as the right and the left side of the heart.[60] The dualism between right and left is exemplified even better by the kidneys: "The reins instruct, the heart understands, the mouth decides"; and the nature of this instruction is made clear when the same text says: "Man has two kidneys, the one counseling good, the other evil." [61] A prayer recorded in the Talmud,[62] and included in the daily prayerbook, says: "May the good inclination and not the evil inclination prevail over me, and make my inclination [63] serve thee, and may I cleave to the good inclination."

We cannot enter more closely here into the metaphysical questions concerning the nature of good and evil which these quotations provoke. The commandment that one should love God with both inclinations, and the prayer for divine assistance in making the evil inclination serve him, show that the suppression or annihilation of "evil" is considered only as an expedient and is in any case inferior to the ideal, though generally unattainable, aim of transforming—or dare we say sublimating?—the evil inclination. The Palestinian Talmud records that Abraham "made the evil inclination good. David, unable to master the evil inclination, had to strike it dead." [64]

We shall confine ourselves, therefore, to those aspects of the rabbinic theory from which we can gain a better understanding of conscience. From the majority of these rabbinic state-

55. Deut. 6:5.
56. Mishnah Berakoth IX. 5.
57. That is, desire and sight.
58. B. Berakoth 1:3c.
59. Num. Rabbah XVII.
60. For instance, Yalkut on Ecclesiastes 10:2: "A wise man's heart is at his right hand" (this means the good inclination), "but a fool's heart is at his left" (this is the evil inclination).
61. B. Berakoth 61a.
62. *Ibid.*, 60b.
63. "Inclination" without further qualification = the evil inclination.
64. B. Berakoth IV.

ments it is quite evident that the "evil inclination" is simply the libido—vital energy in the broadest sense, though in the narrower sense it is the sexual instinct. The theory of the two inclinations accords very well with this thoroughly Platonic motif, which, for aught we know, may actually have been taken over by the rabbis from Platonism. Since the rational interpretation of the good inclination as a regulative principle does not fit the picture of instinct or drive in general, we may suppose that the two "inclinations" embody the nobler and the baser passions. They would then correspond exactly to Plato's two horses.[65] It was inevitable, however, that drives and vital energy would sooner or later be equated with the evil inclination. Paradoxically, when viewed in the perspective of rabbinic thinking, this does not mean that instinct and vital energy are absolutely evil, but, on the contrary, that "evil" is not bad in itself but becomes so only in the specific dimension of human existence. At the conclusion of his work of creation "God saw every thing that he had made, and, behold, it was very good." [66] "Very good," comments the midrash,[67] "by that is meant the evil inclination, for had the evil inclination not existed, no man had built a house and no man had married a wife." A delightfully ironical Talmudic legend tells us that when the rabbis had one day succeeded in catching the (personified) evil inclination and chaining it up, the next day not so much as a fresh egg could be found even for a sick man, so they had to let the evil inclination—indispensable for cocks and men alike—go free again. The evil inclination is innate, and the rabbinic discussion is solely concerned with whether it is operative from the moment of conception or only from birth.[68] Thus, if the evil inclination is innate in man's nature, it is only in man that nature is evil; for "beasts have no evil inclination," [69] although they live a purely natural life.

---

65. *Phaedrus* 246, 253–54.
66. Gen. 1:31.
67. Gen. Rabbah IX.
68. B. Niddah 30b.
69. Gen. Rabbah XIV and Aboth de R. Nathan XVI.

The significant thing about this theory of the two inclinations, from the standpoint of the history of religion, is the psychological interpretation of the dualism of good and evil, which was, no doubt, originally understood in a metaphysical sense. The radical form of dualism, as we know it in the Parsee religion, had already been rejected by the prophets: "I form the light, and create darkness; I make [good], and create evil; [70] I the Lord do all these things," [71] and it appears in a correspondingly milder form in the teachings of the pre-Gnostic Jewish sects. Thus the theology of the Essenes—or, to be more accurate, the sect [72] to which we owe the Dead Sea Scrolls—was governed by the belief in two spiritual realms, both of them created by God and given dominion by him. The prince of light and the spirit of impurity, looked at from a logical point of view, are metaphysical hypostases of the good and evil inclinations. Historically considered, however, the contrary is probably truer: the good and evil inclinations were shifted onto the psychological plane by the rabbis, who thereby took a further step in the direction of rendering the abhorred metaphysical dualism harmless.

As a matter of fact, in the psychological system of the rabbis the good inclination does not appear right from the start as a twin phenomenon together with the evil inclination but emerges as the product of a specifically human psychological development from—and in opposition to—the background of purely natural instinct. That bundle of instincts and reflexes we call an infant begins developing from the first moment of its existence into a human being, that is, into a creature equipped with a conscience (including consciousness, differentiated experience of the outer and inner world, superego, etc.). In the language of the rabbis, this fact of developmental psychology is expressed by saying that the good inclination only appears at a late date. This good inclination—the Jewish con-

70. [For "good," AV has "peace"; RSV "weal." For AV "evil," RSV has "woe."—TRANSLATOR.]
71. Isaiah 45:7.
72. The identity of the two groups is still disputed by many scholars.

science, as we might call it—naturally bears a special relationship to the divine Law, the Torah. No doubt this conception is
deeply rooted in the fundamental religious attitude of the
Bible, an attitude which, equally removed from the pagan
affirmation of life as from its denial, can be described, theologi-
cally as well as psychologically, as a *sanctification of life*. The
good inclination thus becomes a kind of regulative principle by
means of which man consciously, i.e., through his conscience,
subjugates his nature, or the evil inclination—masters it, inte-
grates it, and sanctifies it according to his individual capacities.

Two sets of motifs overlap here, both going back to the
above-mentioned identification of the Torah with Sophia or
Wisdom. The good inclination, say the rabbis, appears in man
when he is thirteen years old. The idea that it awakens only at
puberty and that, consequently, the proverbially "pure" age of
childhood is wholly under the domination of the evil inclination, is remarkable enough in itself. It shows quite clearly that
the essence of the good inclination consists in a growing
distance and detachment from oneself at the onset of maturity.
At thirteen a boy is *bar mizvah*—of religious age—and takes
upon himself the "yoke of the Law." As a child he was free;
and if he was urged to religious practice by parents and
teachers, this was only for pedagogic reasons, by way of
training and instruction, as a preparation for his thirteenth
birthday, when, having come of religious age, he must accept
the discipline of Jewish life. It is quite clear that in this view
the Torah is to be equated with the good inclination. But how
very much the apologetic wish can be father to a tendentious
interpretation is evident from a curious and revealing mistrans-
lation of a midrashic comment on Ecclesiastes 4:14.[73] The
verse "For out of prison he cometh to reign" is interpreted by
the rabbis as referring to the good inclination, since it "comes
to reign" only after the thirteenth year. "Until he is thirteen

73. Cf. *Hamburgers Realencyklopädie für Bibel und Talmud* (Leipzig,
1901), Vol. II, *s.v.* "Gewissen."

the child can do what he likes, *and no one restrains him;* afterwards he is subject to the penalties of the Law." The italicized passage is erroneously translated "and no inner voice holds him back"—an instructive example of the determination to read modern European concepts of morality into Judaism at all costs.

The Talmud [74] puts the following words into God's mouth: "Though I created the evil inclination, I also created an antidote to it in the Torah." The Torah is the order revealed by God, and to know this order is the "conscience" of the Jew. Paraphrasing Jaspers' formulation of the moral conscience,[75] we might say that into the life of the Jew there enters the reality of the Torah, through which he has to acknowledge or reject what should become his being.

The other motif, which overlaps with that of the *bar miz-vah*, originates in the philosophical rationalism we mentioned earlier. Because the Torah can be conceived as the essence of divine reason and hence as accessible to human reason, the awakening of the good inclination can also be understood as the awakening of reason in the maturing youth. The saying, "The evil inclination is thirteen years older than the good inclination," [76] or the somewhat obscure verse about the old king and the young ruler,[77] which is interpreted as an allegory of the older, evil inclination and the younger, good one,[78] can easily be taken in this sense. Indeed, for Bahya ibn Pakuda, the late awakening of the divine gift of reason explains its weakness in the face of the more primitive and therefore more powerful instincts and lusts. This also explains why reason alone is not enough and needs the support of the divinely revealed Law.[79] It is just the contemplative mystic Bahya who, on this point, shows himself altogether in line with the "intel-

---

74. B. Kiddushin 30b.
75. *Supra*, p. 86.
76. Aboth de R. Nathan XVI.
77. Eccles. 4:13–14.
78. B. Nedarim 32a.
79. Bahya ibn Pakuda, "The Book of the Duties of the Heart," III, 2.

lectualism characteristic of the Jewish mentality," [80] especially in his classical "Dialogue between Reason and the Soul." [81] The soul (Arab. *nafs*) here stands for man as a vital phenomenon, a vessel of bodily appetites and drives, while reason, the Neoplatonic *nous*, is a stranger in this world, a wanderer from the spiritual, celestial regions. *Reason is conscience*, which brings the soul to a knowledge of the truth and constrains it, in accordance with this knowledge, to turn its back on the material world and devote itself entirely to the spiritual life. Where the midrash says, "The ungodly are ruled by their heart, but the righteous rule their heart," [82] the medieval thinker would have to translate the rabbinic imagery ("heart-man") into the conceptual pair "soul-reason" in order to make sense of this statement.

The two equations—of the good inclination with reason, on the one hand, and with obligation to the Law, on the other—have one thing in common: universal validity.[83] Both the Torah conscience and the rational conscience are a knowledge, present in man, of an objective, universally valid order, which lays claim to his obedience not as a unique individual but as a member of the species Man or—more precisely—Jew. Conscience can only acknowledge and bear witness to an existing order and, to quote Aquinas again, "bind or incite and also accuse or rebuke" in relation to it. Anything else would contradict reason as well as the binding force of the revealed order. Insofar as the individual conscience seems to open the door to antinomianism, it is an evil conscience,[84] a "whoring-

---

80. G. Vajda, *La teologia ascetica de Bahya ibn Paquda* (1950), p. 41, n. 2.

81. Magisterially analyzed by I. Heinemann, *Die Lehre von der Zweckbestimmung des Menschen im griechisch-römischen Altertum und im jüdischen Mittelalter* (1926), pp. 37 ff., and by Vajda, *op. cit.*, Chap. 4.

82. Gen. Rabbah XXXIV.

83. With the limitation that Jewish theology in general is exclusively concerned with the Jews.

84. Not a "bad conscience" as we understand it, since this is one of the positive functions of the moral conscience. The "evil" conscience is the thought and desire springing from one's own (wicked) heart or from demonic inspiration.

after" the eyes (temptations from outside) and the heart (the selfish conscience).[85]

IV

IT IS PROBABLY NO ACCIDENT that the individualistic tendency in the matter of conscience breaks through at that point in Judaism where a latent (and at times not so latent) antinomianism actually lurks in the background: in the Kabbalah. The point of this breakthrough is not the Kabbalistic theory of the good and evil inclinations, since the Kabbalah hypostatizes the rabbinic psychological concepts back into metaphysical entities again. The "demonization" of evil had, in part, already been prepared in the Talmud, in a splendid equation that combines all the main negative symbols: the evil inclination (tempter) = Satan (accuser) = angel of death (executioner).[86] The Kabbalistic doctrine of the demonic counterrealm of the "other side" does, as a matter of fact, go to the limit of what monotheism can tolerate. However, it is not here that we can gain anything for an understanding of conscience, but rather in the specific psychology of the Kabbalah, i.e., its doctrine of the soul. What dangerously explosive material lies hidden even in the orthodox Kabbalah has been shown by Scholem[87] and his school.[88] The antinomian excesses of the heretical Kabbalah, which—as happens so often in the history of religion—purported to be dictated by a higher, charismatic "conscience," did not drop out of the blue.

It is not possible, within the limits of this essay, to go at all deeply into the Kabbalistic doctrine of the soul.[89] Suffice it to say that the soul is viewed as an organism consisting of 613

85. Num. 15:39: ". . . and that ye seek not after your own heart and your own eyes, after which ye use to go a whoring."
86. B. Baba Bathra 16a.
87. G. Scholem, *Major Trends in Jewish Mysticism* (New York, 1946), pp. 287–324, and *Sabbatai Zwi*, 2 vols. (Tel Aviv, 1957).
88. Especially I. Tishby, *The Doctrine of Evil and the Kelippah in Lurian Kabbalism* (in Hebrew, 1942).
89. Cf. Scholem, "Seelenwanderung und Sympathie der Seelen in der jüdischen Mystik," *Eranos-Jahrbuch XXIV*, 1955 (Zurich, 1956).

"limbs," which constitute the true stature of man. The 613 limbs are derived from the old rabbinic anatomy, where, divided into two groups of 248 and 365, they corresponded to the 248 commandments and 365 prohibitions of the Torah. This anatomical image of the "man-likeness" of the Torah and the "Torah-likeness" of man is interpreted mystically by the Kabbalists: each commandment or prohibition corresponds to a limb of the soul. Only by fulfilling all the commandments of the Torah does fallen man follow the path that leads his imperfect and "crippled" soul to perfection and wholeness. The way is long; the end cannot possibly be reached in a single lifetime, so several reincarnations are needed. It follows, from this view, that in every life a very specific task, appropriate to the individual fate of the soul, awaits realization.

In reality, however, the Kabbalistic theory is much more complicated than this. All souls come from the great primordial soul of the Cosmic Adam, whose full stature of 613 limbs contains the total stock of human souls. For each limb of the mystic Adam itself consists of a further 613 limbs or "soul roots," and each of these is in turn divided into a larger or smaller number of "soul sparks." These sparks, or sub-limbs of the great Adam's psychic organism to the second and third degree, are the actual individual souls whose migrations through the bodies inhabiting our earthly world constitute the true essence of history, which is sacred history. Every soul has, from the beginning of things, another *topos* or "station" in the divine realm, a definite point within the structure of the primordial Anthropos, where it has its unique and individual home in this *corpus mysticum;* and thither, after the Fall, it must find its way back again, if it and the *corpus mysticum* are to be restored to perfection. It goes without saying that no two souls can follow the same path or have the same task. One gets the impression from a reading of the Kabbalistic literature that this individual "soul spark," the true essence of man, expresses itself in a kind of instinctive urge to perform certain actions and to undergo certain experiences. The inadequacy of the universal and the necessity of the individual way are trenchantly expressed in a Hasidic tale, which, in its naïve spirituality, soars over the precipice of anarchic possibilities it has opened up without, apparently, being aware of them:

> Rabbi Baer of Radoshitz once said to his teacher, the rabbi of Lublin: "Show me one general way to the service of God!" The *zaddik* replied: "It is impossible to tell men what way they should take. For one way to serve God is through the teachings, another through prayer, another through fasting, and still another through eating. Everyone should carefully observe what way his heart draws him to, and then choose this way with all his strength." [90]

Nevertheless, the Lurian Kabbalah was obsessed by the eschatological desire to bring sacred history to its end and consummation by restoring as many souls as possible to their original perfection (*tiqqun*). Hence, too, the significant role of charismatically gifted Kabbalists who, by their knowledge of physiognomy and other signs, were able to "read" a man's "soul root" and thus discover his individual task. Rabbi Moses Zacuto, a prominent seventeenth-century Kabbalist, put it thus: "It is the duty of every man to learn to know the root of his soul, so as to perfect it and restore it to its origin, that is, to its essential being. In this way he will find that, to the extent he perfects himself, he progressively comes closer to himself." [91]

Everyone must seek the mystery of his own individuality, and only the man who knows his "root" can come to himself. The Torah is valid for all equally, but everyone has one special point in the organism of the Torah which is valid for his individual "soul spark" in particular. It is but a short step from asserting the particular validity of one particular point in the Torah to declaring certain other points less valid or even nonvalid. One more step and the claim may be made that what is negatively judged and definitely forbidden in general may be positively required of a particular individual. However, these ideas concerning the uniquely individual task of man, as they

---

90. Martin Buber, *Tales of the Hasidim* (London, 1956), p. 313.
91. Cited in Shalom Busaglo, *Mikdash Melekh* (Amsterdam, 1750), p. 132a.

were developed in the Kabbalah and in Hasidism, never led to a theory of conscience: the unquestioned validity and binding force of the Law were too powerful. The use or misuse to which the inner conscience could be put by heretical mystics as well as by assimilationist reformers was not conducive to the development of a genuine doctrine of conscience in Jewish theology. To the extent that the notion crops up at all in modern Jewish literature, it appears as a borrowing from the stock of European culture, as a foreign body to be assimilated rather than as an authentic fruit from the tree of Judaism.

V

IN OUR SOMEWHAT FORMAL SURVEY of conscience in the history of Jewish thought, we were in danger of overlooking one essential point, and that is the material rather than the formal aspects of the matter—in other words, the actual contents of the Jewish conscience in the history of Judaism. For there is no doubt that the Jew was always presented by his conscience with certain definite contents of a moral nature. These contents, in order to become really binding for him, had to be integrated with his *conscientia* by way of certain theological and philosophical patterns of thought (e.g., goodness and rightness as obedience to God's revealed will, as divine Law and Wisdom). But this did not prevent them from continually changing in accordance with autonomous social and historical laws and in their turn bringing about changes of outlook in theology and philosophy. A discussion of the contents of the Jewish conscience and of its changes throughout history does not come within the scope of this essay and must be left to more competent historians and sociologists. Yet even our formal review would be incomplete if we did not pay attention to the attitudes which appeared in the course of Jewish history and were evidently dictated by an authority for which we have no other word but "conscience." Moral conscience manifests itself again and again, beginning with Abraham's appeal to God's conscience not to destroy Sodom: "Wilt thou also destroy the righteous with the wicked?" [92] and so to Job, accusing God, yet trustfully crying out: "God has put me in the wrong [93] . . . [yet] I know that my vindicator lives," [94] right up to the later modifications of the Halakhah. It was just in the post-prophetic period, the period of the Second Temple, that the Halakhic type of piety coined concepts like *hasiduth* ("conscientiousness" going beyond the letter of the Law in dealing with God and man), the "heavenly Law" (a Law of conscience going beyond the religious Law, comparable to the *agraphos nomos* of the Stoics), and the ideal of "keeping *deep within* the Law" (*lifenim mi-shurath ha-din*), as contrasted with the religion of the average man, who is content to keep strictly to "the line of the Law." In the course of time the contents and norms of conscience became constant factors recognized by religious law and integrated into the Halakhic system. The very vagueness of certain biblical commandments, such as "Ye shall be holy," [95] could lead to the insight that a man might "live according to the law of the Torah and still be a villain." [96]

Granted all this, it must nevertheless be emphasized that in order to become moral certitudes within Judaism, and to impose themselves with the force of which conscience is capable, all religious and ethical contents had to present themselves in very definite forms. There is, in the first place, the relationship to a personal God who makes demands on man by the revelation of his will. This relationship calls for responsibility and obedience ("responding" and "hearing") on the part of man. God's will can be heard as an outer or inner voice (as in the revelation on Sinai, or in prophecy), but ultimately it was accessible only through institutionalized authority: through the scribes and rabbis as the qualified interpreters of the Law. The Jewish conscience is Jewish—if we take the adjective in

92. Gen. 18:23.
93. Job 19:6 (RSV).
94. Job 19:25 (RSV).
95. Lev. 19:2.
96. Moses Nahmanides, Commentary on the Pentateuch, *ad loc.*

neither a dogmatic nor racial but a purely empirical and historical sense—because it is anchored in Judaism as a social, historical, and spiritual reality. If being a Jew can by definition mean
nothing else than belonging, and knowing oneself as belonging,
to a particular community, then a Jewish conscience is one that
is bound up with this fact of Jewish existence. For the Bible
this meant the knowledge, vouchsafed by God's revealed Law,
of right conduct and of salvation. The Law is the absolute,
numinous command which, devoid of any anthropocentricity,
addresses itself to the Jew by reason of his being a member of
the chosen community. The command is addressed to the
individual, but it reaches him via the community, the *ecclesia*
Israel. The biblical covenant became the rabbinic Law, and this
—very much rationalized by the medieval philosophers—
turned into a rational order embracing man, world, and Torah.
Conscience, however, has room to play only *within the Law*,
and, as we have seen from the *lifenim mi-shurath ha-din* formula, any conscientious action going beyond the minimal requirements does not go "beyond" the Law in the sense of
"transcending" it but, on the contrary, is regarded as penetrating more deeply within the Law, and as a fuller realization of
its immanent norm. To transgress the "line of the Law" is of
the devil. The one passage in the Talmud [97] in praise of "sinning for a good purpose" remains unique. And because mysticism, in its search for the mystery of the individual, also
discovered the possibility of relativizing or even transcending
the Law, it came in some of its manifestations to the very limit
of Judaism. Antinomianism, which in heretical mysticism was
still a genuinely religious phenomenon, appeared in the age of
secular enlightenment as the dictate of an ethical conscience. In
its formal aspects this conscience had affinities with medieval
rational conceptions, but on the practical side it arrived at very
different conclusions: for now, in the name of conscience, the
traditional body of Jewish religious law could no longer be
accepted (or no longer accepted *in toto*).

97. B. Nazir 23b.

This brings us to the conflicts of conscience in modern Judaism. It is a Judaism into which the twentieth century, with its mass extermination of Jews, the end of the Exile, and the founding of the state of Israel with all its social, political, and spiritual problems, has introduced a fateful change. What this change will signify for the Jewish conscience, and how the transformation of this conscience will in turn transform Judaism, are questions upon which we must leave the historian of the future to pass judgment.

A Protestant View
of Conscience

Hans Schär

*Translated by R. F. C. Hull
and Ruth Horine*

AT THE TURN of the nineteenth century it was popularly believed that religious freedom and freedom of conscience were one of the great blessings of humanity and that freedom of conscience began with the Reformation. Martin Luther's stand at the Diet of Worms seemed to mark the breakthrough for freedom of conscience, when, upholding his point of view against state and church, he is said to have declared: "Here I stand, I can no other!" At that moment, Luther broke with the authorities of his time, state and church, which are still considered authorities today. He had nothing to back him but his own conscience. Thus the Diet of Worms witnessed the advent of the man who knew he was committed solely to his conscience and who mobilized freedom of conscience against all secular and spiritual authorities.

This conception of Luther's Reformation had to be revised at several essential points during the early part of the twentieth century. For one thing, critical research into the history of the Diet of Worms established that there is no definite historical evidence for Luther's words, which for a long time had been a banner for a sort of jingoistic Protestantism. However, it transpired that Luther did in fact maintain his position—even if somewhat hesitantly—and did assert that no one should be compelled to accept a faith against his own conscience and conviction. The appeal to commitment to conscience was certainly made, though not in the dramatic and theatrical style so

113

dear to the nineteenth century, as though Luther were writing his own epitaph. What he actually said was something like this: "If I were not convinced by the testimonies of the Holy Scriptures or on obvious grounds—for I do not believe the pope and the synods alone, since it is certain that they have frequently erred and contradicted themselves—I am bound by the Scriptural texts I have cited, and my conscience is a prisoner of God's word. I cannot, and I will not, recant, for to act contrary to conscience is neither safe nor honorable. So help me God, Amen." [1]

But now we come to another point, which is of crucial importance. While it is true that Luther did act from the compulsion and commitment of his own conscience at the Diet of Worms, he expressly refrained from putting freedom of conscience into effect later on. In the first place, he did not enlist freedom of conscience in his own work of reforming theology and founding the Protestant church. Also, he did not appeal to his own conscience any more but wanted his actions to be determined solely by the Bible. He intended to carry out a reform of the church according to the clear and definite precepts of the Scriptures and not according to the dictates of his own conscience or that of his supporters. The purpose of his reform was a restoration of the true Christian faith, and the church he founded, when reform of the Catholic church proved impossible, was to be the original and now restored Christian church and community. He did not appeal to conscience to justify this reform, unmindful of the fact that by appealing to his own conscience he had launched the Reformation.

There is a second important reason why the further course of the Reformation left little room for freedom of conscience. The struggle with the Counter Reformation launched by the Catholic church resulted in a Protestant orthodoxy, increasingly rigid and sternly committed to established principles.

---

1. Quoted from R. Huch, *Das Zeitalter der Glaubensspaltung* (Zurich, 1937), p. 115.

Even later, the Reformation did not allow believers freedom of decision in matters of faith but adopted the principle of *cuius regio, eius religio,* which meant that, both by law and in practice, the confessional allegiance of the ruler determined that of his subjects and of the entire region. In Protestant and Catholic territories alike, the ruler ensured the uniformity of religious belief. Consequently, not only Catholicism was attacked in the Protestant countries but various sects as well, such as the Baptists, and—strangest of all—a campaign was even waged against other Protestant denominations. Protestants with a Lutheran bent were expelled from Switzerland, and it remains a thoroughly unsettling fact that Lutherans did not tolerate Zwinglians and Calvinists and even punished them with death. For a long time a sword was kept in Saxony with which crypto-Calvinists were executed. It bore the appropriate inscription *cave Calviniste* ("Calvinist, beware!"). Obviously, this internecine religious intolerance abolished the very idea of freedom of conscience.

From this brief review of the development of the Reformation some important inferences may be drawn which are relevant to our theme. First, conscience is a reality that continually makes its presence felt in practical life. Second, the precise definition of the essence of conscience proves to be extraordinarily difficult. Third, it is evident that in the sphere of religion conscience does not always have a constant, uniform function but subsists in a relation of reciprocal influence with other psychic and spiritual factors by which it is continually modified.

Hence we are obliged to reflect upon what conscience really is from the Protestant point of view, how it is evaluated, and what its function is in the general context of human behavior.

The concept of conscience in German occurs for the first time in the writings of Notker[2] as *gewizzide* or *gewizzani,* a

2. [Notker the Biglipped (Labeo), also called the German (Teutonicus), *ca.* 950–1022, of the monastery of St. Gall, Switzerland. He translated a large number of Latin writers into Old High German and is therefore a source for many philosophical and theological terms in

literal translation of the Latin *conscientia*, which in turn was derived from the Greek *syneidēsis*. The concept is pre-Christian; indeed the very term was coined by the Greeks and Romans. There are, however, indications that the phenomenon itself, conscience as a psychospiritual function, had already developed among the ancient Egyptians. For them a functioning conscience was inherent in the nature of man, though the concept as such did not yet exist. According to the histories of philosophy, it played but a minor role in Greek thought too, for Greek writers mostly mention only that people can have a bad conscience that torments them, perhaps even more severely than social censure and punishment. It was Cicero, Livy, and Pliny the Younger who elaborated the concept by speaking not only of a bad but also of a good conscience.

Passing on to the Christian era, we must ask what is said about conscience in the Bible. In Hebrew and thus in the Old Testament there is no word for conscience. In the Septuagint, the Greek translation of the Old Testament, the Greek term for conscience is used only once as the translation of a Hebrew word (Eccles. 10:20).[3] Conscience is also mentioned once in The Wisdom of Solomon 17:11, but this is part of the Apocrypha and not a canonical book. Although the concept of conscience does not occur in the Old Testament, the phenomenon itself emerges very clearly, for instance in the story of Cain and Abel and, more particularly, of the Fall. Cain's defiant question, "Am I my brother's keeper?" (Gen. 4:9) clearly expresses a bad conscience. But the story of the Fall is even more interesting and instructive. Adam and Eve are seduced into eating the apple by the serpent's promise "ye shall be as gods, knowing good and evil" (Gen. 3:5). Taken literally, this

---

German. His use of "conscience" first appears in OHG in his translation of the Psalms. Cf. *Die Religion in Geschichte und Gegenwart*, 3d rev. ed., ed. K. Galling *et al.* (Tübingen: J. C. B. Mohr [Paul Siebeck], 1957–65), articles on Notker, Vol. IV, p. 1532, by H. Beumann, and on "Gewissen," Vol. II, p. 1551, by E. Wolff.—Editor.]

3. ["Curse not the king, no not in thy thought" (Authorized Version). "Thought" also in Douai and Revised Standard and Soncino versions. Cf. note 25a in the preceding essay.—Translator.]

implies that the purpose of the Fall was what we commonly suppose to be the function of conscience: discrimination between good and evil. This raises the question whether the Fall was really so bad, so sinful. However, the seduction includes the rider "ye shall be as gods" and hence also the element of *hybris*. The consequence of the Fall is shame, and it is a sexual shame, for Adam and Eve cover their sexual parts. Whether they reached the promised goal as a result of the Fall is not made very clear, but the fact that they are ashamed is evidence enough of their bad conscience. They hide from God.

Another feature of this story is that although God punished man for transgressing his commandment, he apparently allowed him to keep his knowledge of good and evil (Gen. 3:22). And in the story of the Flood, which follows, it is noteworthy that God did not restore the paradisal *status quo ante* but left man also with his knowledge of shame (Gen. 9:21–23). We are left in the dark as to whether the consequence of the Fall was the awakening of conscience as a vital function or whether it was merely the first awakening of a bad conscience. Should the latter interpretation be accepted, the promise of the serpent would be superbly ironical, for in effect it would be saying: "After eating of the Tree of Knowledge, you shall know good and evil by having a bad conscience." But the story can be given yet another twist: only through sin, through violating a divine commandment, does man realize that he has a conscience. The only way of knowing that we have a conscience is in the experience of personal guilt. At all events, it is plain that more is known about conscience in the Old Testament than the purely philological evidence allows, according to which there is no word for conscience in Hebrew.

In the New Testament the philological picture is quite different. Here we find two Greek terms, *synoida* and *syneidēsis*, both taken from common usage and of long standing. The literal meaning of *syneidēsis* is "knowledge with," which was later interpreted as "knowledge with God." But at the time of the New Testament it is certain that it had not yet been construed in this way. The prefix *syn-*, or Latin *con-*, implies connection, combination, union. Hence *syneidēsis*, derived from *syneidos* (literally, "seeing with or together"), is a synthetizing kind of knowledge or understanding, unifying the multiplicity of perceptions into a spiritual awareness or self-awareness. The term can also be applied to moral consciousness, or man's evaluation of himself by means of his self-awareness. In Christian usage *syneidēsis* is the inner awareness of God and his order, awareness of sin as a violation of this order for which no outer acts can atone. Man's *con-scientia* bears joint witness to the law of God that is written in the heart, even though his thoughts may be in profound conflict with one another. Conscience is thus the expression of man's inner awareness, with special reference to ethical conduct. With these conceptions of conscience Christianity hardly contributed anything new to the times. More important was the Christian insistence on a good conscience, which in the New Testament is often described as Christianity's essential gift to man, along with faith. Attention is paid not only to bad conscience resulting from the commission of an evil deed but also to good conscience as our awareness of having done good and eschewed evil.

In this connection it may be of interest to cite some further references in the New Testament. A text that lays particular emphasis on the function of conscience is the parable of the Prodigal Son (Luke 15:11 ff.). Actually, the son does not break any specific commandment, except possibly the general one of filial piety. When the son asks for his inheritance, his father gives it to him without protest or reprimand. His insight, or bad conscience, is awakened only after he has squandered his fortune and has found himself in difficult straits, owing partly to his evil ways and partly to the hard times (widespread famine). Here the transgression is not so much the breaking of a commandment as the son's selfish and disrespectful behavior toward his father, who stands for God. To us this would probably seem less striking and indeed revolutionary than it did to the Jews at that time, who were brought up in fidelity to the Law and for whom disobedience to the Law was synonymous with sin.

To grasp the full significance of the New Testament statements about conscience we must also take baptism into account. Baptism, as the bath of rebirth, signified the death of the old man and the resurrection of the new. Among other rewards, it brought forgiveness of sins. Before being baptized, the candidate made a full confession of sin and promised to lead a sinless life from then on. He was then accepted into the community of the saints. This conception of baptism arose in connection with the anticipation of an imminent end of the world, for in the first centuries of our era the coming of the Kingdom of God was expected daily. The obligation to lead a sinless life was taken very seriously by the early Christians. They were also convinced that a sinless life and the assurance of forgiveness were possible only through faith. Faith brought trust in, and participation in, the coming Kingdom of God, as well as the infusion of the Holy Spirit, who would lend them moral strength and enable them to overcome sin as the temptation of Satan and the Antichrist. Thus a good conscience was possible in the context of a given historical situation and under the impact of experiences which were connected with baptism and the early Christians' experience of the spirit. But these experiences had by then reached a climax and could not long be maintained at that level of intensity.

Baptism brought forgiveness of sins but was possible only once in a lifetime. Then two things happened—or rather, did not happen. The imminently expected Kingdom of God failed to appear, and, instead of being strengthened, spiritual experiences took a different turn and became less intense. A crucial change was obviously in the making, because the sinless life originally demanded of the baptized was turning out to be impossible. Before long, the Christian communities had to face the question of what to do with people who had been baptized and yet continued to sin. At first, the demands for a sinless life were mitigated by making a distinction between forgivable and unforgivable, or venial and mortal, sins. As time went on, this

led to the institution of penitence, or confession. Thus the
church became a veritable therapeutic institute, since it controlled the door to salvation. The striking thing about the
institution of confession is not only that the connection between the gift of faith and the forgiveness of sins through
baptism was broken but that, above all, the authority of the
church increasingly took the place of conscience. It was the
church that decided, more and more obviously and explicitly,
what was good and evil and what was merit and sin. Regard
for conscience was pushed into the background.

While it is not possible for us to outline here the whole
development of conscience throughout the history of Christianity, we should at least like to draw attention to two contri-
butions made by Saint Augustine. First of all, he had a strong
sense of his personal guilt, which he acknowledged to the full.
In his *Confessions* he made a matchless confession of it in the
form of a prayer. Even as a bishop, the head of a community
with great authority, he frankly and openly revealed his entire
personal life and his sinful inclinations. The judgment he pronounced on himself was in fact a clear judgment of conscience,
and he acknowledged it as such without reservation. His pro-
cedure marks an advance in the recognition of conscience.

Saint Augustine's second contribution is the doctrine of
original sin. Rigorously elaborated under the influence of Man-
ichaeism, it states that man is incapable of good. Fallen man
cannot avoid sinning (*non potest non peccare*). Original sin is
automatically transmitted to every man by heredity, through
physical procreation and his physical nature in general. Therefore, everything the natural man does is sin and only sin. Saint
Augustine did not even ask himself whether recognition of sin
does not presume at least a good insight and some capacity for
good. He obviously used the doctrine of original sin to bind
man even more closely to the church. Only baptism can de-
liver man from original sin, and only the church can administer
baptism. In order to avoid being an eternal prisoner of evil,
man has to submit to the authority of the church. Coupled

with this is the demand for an ascetic life, which Saint Augustine valued above any other.

Saint Augustine's attitude to conscience thus contains a contradiction. On the one hand, more than anyone at that time he sharpened the emphasis on conscience, but on the other hand he demanded man's submission to the authority of the church so emphatically that conscience became practically superfluous, if not ruled out altogether. So it is hardly surprising that the dictum is attributed to Saint Augustine: *Roma locuta, causa finita* ("Rome having spoken, the case is closed"). Actually, he applied this dictum only to one particular case and did not recognize at the outset the authority of the bishop of Rome in all matters. Nevertheless, his thinking and his whole attitude tended in that direction.

Among the various steps in the historical development of conscience during the Middle Ages, we should like to single out only the distinction which the Schoolmen made between *synterēsis* and *conscientia*. The word *synterēsis* appears to derive from a scribal error in Saint Jerome's *Commentary on Ezekiel* (1:7), where it occurs as a corruption of *syneidēsis*. According to the Scholastic view, *conscientia* is the scrutinizing and regulating conscience, while *synterēsis* represents the rational principles of moral action which are inborn in man as the "natural law" by which he should regulate his whole conduct. Accordingly, *synterēsis* would be the general theoretical conscience, while *conscientia* is its practical application in individual cases.

The beginning of the Reformation was marked by a conflict of conscience which Luther experienced while he was in the monastery at Erfurt. Today it is assumed that this conflict arose as a result of Luther's decision to enter the monastery, though his reasons for doing so are not altogether clear. At any rate, he reached this decision without securing the consent of his father, who had entirely different plans for his son. Luther himself claimed that he entered the monastery because of a vow he had made to Saint Anne during a violent thunderstorm near Stotternheim which had endangered his life. The thunderstorm occurred during a journey that was probably connected with his departure, at mid-semester, from the University of Erfurt, when he went home to announce that he no longer intended to study jurisprudence, as his father wished. His father did not agree with this change of plan. It was during this journey that Luther, in real or imaginary danger, suddenly made his vow, probably expressing a long-standing or unconscious wish which he now fulfilled by entering the Augustinian monastery at Erfurt. Luther took this step in the conviction that the storm was a clear sign from God that he should carry out his plan. His novitiate passed without difficulties or temptations; these came only after he had taken his vows and celebrated his first Mass. Something must have happened then that troubled Luther deeply. It may have been the presence of his father, who, on that solemn occasion, had expressed his displeasure at his son's monkishness. When Luther, in self-defense, pointed out that his thunderstorm experience was an act of divine providence and that he was bound by the vow he had made to the saint, his father riposted that obedience to parents also figured among the divine commandments and furthermore that there was no evidence at all that divine providence had been at work—the thunderstorm experience might equally well have been the work of evil spirits or demons. With that Luther was plunged into a profound inner conflict which reduced him to utter despair. In the end he could only suppose that he was completely damned by God.

As a result, Luther was tormented by a conflict of conscience, being confronted with two contradictory obligations both of which he felt duty-bound to fulfill. He also had to admit that decisions of conscience might be precarious; we may think we are obeying our conscience, yet we cannot avoid falling into sin. On top of all that, in the period that followed he was plagued by further difficulties. In his depressed state, he accused himself of every conceivable sin but could find no relief in confession. He was in fact unable to confess anything that would have been sufficient reason for such an abysmal feeling of guilt. His friend and superior, Father Staupitz, is said to have told him that he was confessing the merest trifles. Unless he was able to accuse himself of some really outsize fault, he should put away his guilt feelings. At this time Luther turned into a regular scruple-monger, continually running to the confessional yet unable to unbosom himself of his guilt.

Luther finally regained his peace of mind in the so-called theology of the Cross. This consists in man's humble submission to God's decrees, even though God should reject him. In Luther's view, man's attitude is thus brought into harmony with that of Jesus Christ, who in all humility accepted the Cross and bore it to the end. From the mystic Johann Tauler (d. 1361), Luther took over the similar idea that man, out of love for God, must submit to every divine decree no matter how harsh and damning. If man out of love for God could accept every divine decree, and if out of such love he is even able to resign himself to total rejection and to Hell (*se resignare ad infernum*), then, despite everything, he is not wholly separated from God. In this way Luther arrived at an extremely irrational formula which affirmed at the same time both guilt and bond with God, both distance from God and nearness to him.

Luther's inner development is relevant to our problem, because it shows that conscience and the feeling of guilt operating within it together constitute an important agent in the evolution of his reformatory ideas. It also clarifies the inner reason for his gradual breaking-away from the Catholic church, since in his case confession, offered by the church as a relief from a bad conscience, did not work. It was because the church was unable to cope with conscience that he put his trust in conscience rather than in the church.

But conscience alone did not provide Luther with an answer to his problem. He learned that conscience is a tough prosecutor and that against the verdict of conscience man cannot justify himself even by his ethical behavior. Here faith provides the only answer. For this reason, Luther insisted that man must acknowledge the reality of his bad conscience and guilt feelings. Man is a sinner, and his behavior remains sinful. Saint Augustine had already established this fact, but his solution— an ascetic life and submission to the church as a divine therapeutic institute—was no longer valid for Luther in overcoming sin, for even the ascetic life remains sinful. Torn between two duties, he had personally experienced a conflict of conscience, and he knew that we may become guilty not only through our sins of commission but also through our sins of omission. The ascetic may deny himself as much as is humanly possible, but he still does not escape his guilt. Therefore asceticism is no guarantee of a good conscience. Conscience accuses and must accuse because its accusations are true.

Luther found his answer in faith alone. In love of God, and by accepting himself as he really is, man submits to God's judgment and providence. He does not achieve a good conscience, but at least he recognizes that God's love is stronger than his own guilt and the verdict of his own conscience. Later, as we know, Luther did not stick to the theology of the Cross, but, influenced by the Pauline epistles and by the need to have an authoritative backing for his views, he focused on the doctrine of justification by faith. The theology of the Cross cannot be found either in Paul's letters or in the Gospels. The doctrine of justification by faith does, however, occur in Paul, though in a context very different from the one Luther thought it did. But that was immaterial to Luther; it was enough for him that it occurred in the New Testament. He interpreted it in accordance with Anselm's doctrine of satisfaction, namely, that God through Christ had made sufficient atonement for human sin and that those who believed in Christ would therefore be forgiven. However, Luther modified the effect of God's work of reconciliation at one point: although man may be *declared* righteous through faith, he is not thereby *made* righteous, as was taught by Anselm and the Catholic church. An essential part of the theology of the Cross is thus preserved, the irrational combination of opposites: before his conscience man remains a sinner and is forever unable to satisfy God's law, but before God he is accepted through

God's grace. Thus, according to Luther's irrational formula, man is at the same time sinful and righteous (*simul iustus et peccator*). In other words, Luther accepted the judgment of conscience and rejected any appeasement of it. The function of conscience is to measure man against God's law and continually to make clear to him how far he is removed from any perfection and how much he remains guilty before God in all his doings. For Luther it is not the function of conscience to pronounce the final judgment on man. That is left to God. Man has access to God's judgment through faith.

So it all depends on the context in which Luther spoke about conscience. He had more faith in conscience than in absolution by the Catholic church. At the Diet of Worms he declared that no man should be compelled to accept a belief contrary to his conscience. Yet he seemed almost to make light of the *terrores conscientiae*. He says in effect: if conscience so persecutes you with hair-splittings and guilt feelings that you cannot live any more, then have a good laugh at it and sin boldly. For—so Luther reasoned—Satan or other evil spirits might well be lurking behind the insinuations of conscience. Like Ignatius of Loyola, he had come to the conclusion that a hair-splitting and overscrupulous conscience might well not be the voice of God but the work of the devil. But the essential point for Luther was always man's relation to God. Employing a word which Luther used in a different context, one could say that he judged conscience in every situation according to whether it "promotes" (*treibet*) Christ or not. Whenever conscience served to clarify man's relation to God, Luther wanted it taken carefully and unreservedly into account. But conscience must not come between man and God in a manner calculated to disturb or actually destroy his trust in God and his firm foothold in faith.

Luther's assertions went further than this since he also recognized a good conscience. According to him and other reformers, a good conscience is possible only through God's grace. Grace grants remission of sins, and thus the sinner who admits his guilt overcomes fear. The resulting state of inner peace brings about a good conscience. For Luther a good conscience may be achieved in another way too. The believer who has received God's grace is delivered from fear of sin and possesses the capacity for real love. Whatever comes from love is ethically good. To a certain extent, the believer is capable of doing good, not because of personal merit but because of grace and in gratitude for this grace; and that kind of good action is combined with a good conscience.

We may thus discern in Luther two conceptions of conscience. First, conscience is the faculty of ethical judgment; second, it is a form of awareness, common to all men, that is directly related to religious experience and faith.

Luther's statements concerning the function of conscience clarify much that came to light in the subsequent development of Protestantism. Protestantism has always recognized conscience as a paramount authority. Although Luther's Protestantism created no new conception of conscience, his inner self-reliance and his guidance by the decisions of conscience did succeed in preventing freedom of conscience from disappearing altogether, in spite of increasing orthodoxy. Conscience preserved both of the above-mentioned meanings: the faculty of ethical judgment and the totality of religious knowledge and judgments. It is, of course, possible to interpret Luther as meaning that conscience alone is empowered to judge good and evil, the criterion lying not in man but in the Bible. Conscience thus becomes a purely formal faculty of judgment, intrinsically bound to the Bible and its divine commandments. This is the Bible-bound conscience of the orthodox period, when conscience was directed just as authoritatively as in Catholicism. The Catholic direction of conscience is more accommodating in that the Catholic church recognizes not only the biblical revelation but, in addition, the teaching office, which, by the application of casuistics,[4] largely relieves

4. [The word "casuistics" is used here instead of the theological term "casuistry" to avoid confusion with its other, and more general, connotation: "sophistical, equivocal, or specious reasoning" (Webster). Casuistry in the theological sense is defined as "The art or science of bringing

conscience of its directing role in matters of ethical decision. In time, the orthodox sanction of conscience by the sole authority of the Bible was bound to become questionable, for even the most consistently orthodox person had to choose between the various biblical commandments, and do so moreover on the basis of a personal decision. The Old Testament laws concerning worship and purification were simply impossible to carry out, although in the Old Testament they were considered to be just as important as the ethical commandments. In consequence, the casuistic use of the Bible as a moral authority for conscience was put in question. Pietism and the Enlightenment brought about a turning point. The Enlightenment applied the criterion of reason to biblical pronouncements and commandments and so did not permit the solitary word of the Bible to be the ultimate authority for conscience. For the Pietists, conversion, the living experience of faith, was more important than the usurpation of the biblical word for one's own use.

These developments led to an unshackling of conscience from its bondage to the Bible and the church, and the problem of freedom of conscience emerged once again. In its entry for *Gewissen* (conscience) the new Brockhaus dictionary says that Protestantism began by deriving conscience from the Bible and building it up into a philosophical doctrine but then laid the emphasis on personal responsibility and freedom of conscience. This is also true of Neo-Protestantism. As we have seen, the beginnings of Luther's Reformation fitted this definition, but its continuation was different. Seen in the broad historical and cultural perspective, the Reformation was closely associated with Humanism and the Renaissance. Both defended the cause of freedom of conscience far more energetically and persistently than did the orthodoxy that followed the Reformation. Concern for freedom of conscience re-emerged only in Neo-Protestant times, conscience being de-

---

general moral principles to bear upon particular cases. Its exercise is always called for in moral issues, whether the particular decision is made by individual judgment or in accordance with an established code" (*Oxford Dictionary of the Christian Church*).—TRANSLATOR.]

fined as the totality of man's cognitive and judging faculties. In that case, the goal of freedom of conscience is that man should be able to stand by a particular point of view without qualification, doubt, or *reservatio mentalis*. The oath of office for Protestant ministers in Bern includes an obligation to preach the Gospel purely and honestly, according to their best knowledge and conscience. In other words, no one should preach anything he cannot wholly subscribe to or which would bring him into conflict with his ethical duty to be truthful. Man must have this freedom, since freedom is a necessary condition of truthfulness. This means that the individual must preserve his freedom vis-à-vis all authority. Naturally he can bow to authority if impelled by an insight or conviction of conscience, but that does not absolve him from the obligation to preserve a measure of inner freedom from this authority, nor may he obey at the cost of his individual truthfulness. In the Neo-Protestant view, there is only one absolute authority, God. If an experience is felt to be absolute, we must bow to it. The ethical requirements of the Bible, especially those of Jesus Christ, may be, and often are, experienced as absolutes by Protestants. But these are only guidelines for conscience, and it is not required that truthfulness bow to them. Furthermore, the ethical commandments of the Bible are requirements, not experiences. Absolute experiences occur very rarely, and, such experiences apart, Protestants have the duty to search their conscience scrupulously and take its decisions with the utmost seriousness.

Conscience as a moral judge gave Neo-Protestants considerable cause for reflection. One thing was certain: there could be no room for the method of casuistics. By his commandment to love—a commandment that for him summed up all others—Jesus Christ provided a guideline by which conscience had to decide in each individual case. The question of a good and a bad conscience also arose. Can Christians have a good conscience, or are they always under the pressure of a bad conscience, which they need time and again as a salutary stimulus? Both views have been defended in Protestantism. In his short story "Meretlein," [5] Gottfried Keller denounced the kind of Christianity that is entirely motivated by a bad conscience, which, it is alleged, is indispensable for subjugating man's nature and preparing him for acceptance of the true faith. Another trend in Protestantism lays particular emphasis on the acquisition of a good conscience. Anyone who has the right kind of faith must have a good conscience, as he is on the right road. Conversely, a good conscience is an infallible sign that one possesses the right faith. The doctrine of justification by faith is apt to lead to this emphasis on a good conscience. Revivalist movements usually arouse a bad conscience to begin with; later the time may come when a good conscience and an optimistic view of human behavior get into the running. Fundamentally, though, the same tension which Luther experienced must be held fast and endured: a recognition of the moral insufficiency of all human behavior in the face of an absolute ethical demand. Yet conscience must not be used to abandon man completely to the *terrores conscientiae* and to rob him of all courage and of the very possibility of ethical action. The *terrores conscientiae*, the temptations of conscience, may easily lead to paralysis of the moral will. That is the exact opposite of the true purpose of a bad conscience. On the one hand, the tension is necessary because in many cases ethical action means acting contrary to our natural impulses and strivings. On the other hand, we must always find the courage and strength to dare to do good. Luther knew that the *terrores conscientiae* may be the work of the devil, but Albert Schweitzer was equally justified in postulating that a good conscience may be an invention of the devil too.

In summing up the Protestant view of conscience, the first conclusion we must come to is that conscience is a primordial phenomenon, present in man from the beginning. Yet the phenomenon is a puzzling one, for the fact that there is something in man which can oppose his natural behavior is far from self-evident and is rather a matter for continual amazement.

5. "Little Meret," in *Green Henry*, trans. A. M. Holt (London, 1960).

The second conclusion is that conscience, as a human function, has certain specific tasks to perform. It must therefore be recognized and heeded, as well as being meaningfully integrated into the total personality. Conscience also has a religious function, but it is not the only religious function and must always be coordinated meaningfully with other functions. This coordination must take into account the nature of conscience and what it can give to man but must also consider his inner constellation and the outer circumstances in which he lives. It is the duty of every epoch, indeed of every individual, constantly to reflect anew on the nature, the significance, and the tasks of conscience.

A Catholic View
of Conscience

Josef Rudin

*Translated by R. F. C. Hull
and Ruth Horine*

I s it permissible to speak of a "Catholic view" of conscience if conscience constitutes a universal reality for the entire family of man—a reality as old as mankind itself? Does it make sense to lay stress on such a view if other Christian and non-Christian conceptions are closely related to the Catholic one? Evidently conscience is a very complex phenomenon that does not lend itself to easy or simple elucidation. Despite agreement on fundamental questions, very different conclusions may be drawn in regard, for instance, to freedom of conscience and the education of conscience. We cannot, however, single out and discuss only these differences, since they are not just accidental or determined by merely outside factors but are due to a different understanding of the complex phenomenon itself. It is therefore essential to consider the Catholic viewpoint as a totality, even though it may include questions where agreement with other theories of conscience is self-evident.

The centrality of the problem of conscience is underlined by the volume of Catholic literature that has grown up around this theme in the course of the centuries. It would no doubt be interesting to review the purely historical development of the conception of conscience and to hear what important theologians have had to say on the subject, but this is precluded by limitations of space. What we are concerned with here is the gradual emergence of systematic lines of thought. Furthermore, the Catholic view as such is not identical with the

133

personal conception of conscience held by individual Catholic philosophers or theologians. In all important matters it is always grounded, first, on the doctrines of the church, based in turn on the texts of the Old and New Testament as well as on the tradition of the teaching office, and, second, on a careful consideration of what in the course of thousands of years of human history has crystallized into a *consensus generis humani*.

Before we examine in detail the Catholic understanding of conscience, a preliminary discussion is needed in order to remind ourselves briefly of what we might call "conscience as a given reality." When we come to the understanding of conscience, I should like to proceed along two lines of inquiry, the first concerning itself only with the Catholic concept of man's natural disposition for conscience, the second with conscience as an act of free decision. This latter inquiry will involve an examination of the church's attitude toward the important issues of the erring conscience and freedom of conscience.

A. CONSCIENCE AS A GIVEN REALITY

IF CATHOLIC moral theologians, in accounting for the fact of conscience, base their case primarily on the *consensus generis humani*, they do so not because they are at a loss for an explanation or for reasons of tactical adroitness. Rather, they are expressing a deep-seated conviction that, in essential matters, Catholic thinking acknowledges its intimate relation with the ultimate spiritual depths as humanity at all times and places has understood and surmised them to be and that the highest value should be set on this consensus. The importance of this extremely rare unanimity as to the reality of conscience among all known primitive as well as highly developed cultures can hardly be overestimated. Except for purely materialistic theories, even the most bitterly opposed religious creeds and intrinsically irreconcilable philosophies of life are unanimous in assuming the existence of some inner regulating force, an incorruptible moral principle of action, an infallible spiritual criterion, or a mysteriously operating *daimonion*. Here we are confronted with what the philosophers of the late Middle Ages used to call the immutable nature of man, in whose depths knowledge of right and wrong, of good and evil, is indestructibly anchored and makes itself felt as an inner "voice" which cannot remain unheeded.

The divine revelation proclaimed in the Old and New Testament, therefore, does not address itself to a psychic void from which no echo resounds. Still less is this echo discordant with the voice of human nature. The different voices resounding in the ultimate statements and fundamental requirements of human morality harmonize in a single chord: "Eschew evil, and do good" (1 Peter 3:11). The reader will come across constant variations of this primordial commandment in the Old Testament. There conscience appears as the voice of the "heart" or of the "soul" or simply as an expression of the "inward parts." Job in the depths of humiliation was able to affirm, "My heart shall not reproach me so long as I live" (27:6). Conscience is also experienced as a direct relationship to a personal God who calls to man, as in Genesis when, after slaying his brother, Cain cries out, ". . . from thy face shall I be hid" (4:14). Hence added weight is lent to the spontaneous call of conscience by the simultaneous and unfailing testing of man by God. In innumerable variants the Old Testament confronts man again and again with this incorruptible witness from whom he cannot escape and to whom he must answer for his deeds and his thoughts. The Psalms, to be sure, offer examples also of the false peace and smug contentment of those who, dulled in conscience and hardened in wrongdoing, glory in their success, intoxicated by the criminal sovereignty of a freedom responsible to no one and a law unto itself.[1] Never-

---

1. [Cf. Psalm 73:3-10 (RSV): "I was envious of the arrogant, when I saw the prosperity of the wicked. For they have no pangs; their bodies are sound and sleek. They are not in trouble as other men are; they are not stricken like other men. Therefore pride is their necklace; violence covers them as a garment. Their eyes swell out with fatness, their hearts overflow with follies. They scoff and speak with malice; loftily they threaten oppression. They set their mouths against the heavens, and their

theless, side by side with the morality of the law, imposed from without and binding, the Old Testament recognized an inner morality of conscience. Though emphasis tended to be placed increasingly on the first, the second cannot be overlooked. Here we are concerned only with conscience as a reality, not with the relation between moral law and moral conscience in Judaism.

The jarring and ever-present reality of conscience is not only confirmed in the New Testament but seen in an entirely new light, and it becomes the dominant note of Christ's message. As the central Christian pronouncement, the Sermon on the Mount is shot through with acute tensions of opposites—between the letter of the law and the strength of the heart, an outward parade of morality and the heart's inner thoughts. The struggle against the legalism of the Pharisees assumed proportions and a degree of intensity that are understandable only because the point at issue was one of the most crucial in Christ's message. Christianity introduced a new order, though to begin with it was still embedded in the old. Christ expressed it in the marvelous symbolism of the eye:

> The light of the body is the eye: therefore when thine eye is single, thy whole body also is full of light; but when thine eye is evil, thy body also is full of darkness. Take heed therefore that the light which is in thee be not darkness. If thy whole body therefore be full of light, having no part dark, the whole shall be full of light, as when the bright shining of a candle doth give thee light (Luke 11:34–36).

The eye of conscience is a gift of nature granted also to nonbelievers, who can live righteously with its help, as Paul pointed out at some length in his Epistle to the Romans (2:12–29). But, over and above this, something entirely new, capable of producing revolutionary effects in a truly Christian life, has been added: the principle of the Holy Spirit, whose

---

tongue struts through the earth. Therefore the people turn and praise them; and find no fault in them."—TRANSLATOR.]

function is not only to refine the natural conscience, endowing it with self-assurance and the power of decision, but to "guide you into all truth" (John 16:13) and to "convince the world of sin and of righteousness and of judgment" (John 16:8, RSV).

Thus in the Catholic view conscience is a datum of human nature, reaffirmed, fortified, and rendered more vital by the advent of Christ.

B. The Understanding of Conscience

For Catholic thinking, conscience is characterized by two very different aspects which must be clearly differentiated if it is to be understood from the Catholic point of view. First, we encounter it as a disposition ingrained in man's whole nature, and to this extent conscience is firmly established, binding, mandatory, and without freedom for the Catholic. Second, it manifests itself conclusively as a personal decision arrived at by an act of judgment, and in this sense the conscience of the Catholic is free, profoundly his own, and a matter of individual responsibility.

1. Conscience as a Disposition of Man's Whole Nature

The ultimate foundation of conscience does not come from outside but is inherent in man's innermost being as a structural ground plan and a permanent pattern of order. It is his nature itself, struggling toward the goals of wholeness and harmony and conscious of its obligation to do so. The Schoolmen called it *synderēsis* or, even better, *syneidēsis*, which we may paraphrase as the "natural disposition for conscience." As a result, man feels and knows himself "in the deepest and highest reaches of his soul to be so bound by value that fulfilling the demands of *syneidēsis* gives him strength, health, joy, and peace, but nonfulfillment brings disruption, anxiety, torment, and guilt." [2] What is this natural disposition, looked at more closely? We can hardly imagine anything more comprehensive and all-embracing. In a lengthy address to the Congress of Catholic Psychotherapists in April, 1953, Pope Pius XII dealt exhaustively with this natural disposition as the natural image of man. We cannot reproduce his ideas *in extenso* but shall refer only to those having particular significance for our discussion. Essentially, the natural disposition is characterized by three dimensions: (1) the dimension of the intra-individual, (2) the dimension of social commitment and orientation, and (3) the dimension of transcendental relationship.

1. The Dimension of the Intra-Individual

This includes, first of all, everything relating to what is currently designated the "conscience of biological fitness" [3]—the innate drive of the somatic organism to develop, its various warning signals, its need for a healthy state of equilibrium. The "psychic conscience" penetrates much deeper and legitimately demands the development of all psychic forces and functions, on the conscious as well as the unconscious level, in accordance with their nature. The investigations of depth psychology into the various determinisms, mechanisms, and the whole dynamism of the psyche were highly appreciated by Pius XII. However, the prime requisite which the ecclesiastical authorities stress and insist on is the quite specific recognition of the spiritual disposition as well. This cannot be considered a mere *quantité négligéable* in the intrapsychic structure but must be acknowledged as the guiding and orienting organ of the psyche itself. While no elementary instinctual drive can lay legitimate claim to this leading role, the spiritual organ is normally in a position to exercise this inner guidance. We must not assume that psychic disturbances are the norm. Panpsy-

2. B. Häring, *Das Gesetz Christi: Moraltheologie* (Freiburg i.B., 1954), p. 187.
3. [Cf. below, Blum's essay, n. 4, relating to Monakow's definition of *hormē*.—TRANSLATOR.]

chologism is just as one-sided and therefore just as erroneous as its opposite, Rousseauesque naturalistic optimism.

The intrapsychic dimension of man's natural disposition therefore presents a very complex picture, and one can well understand why this disposition has been given so many names, most of which express only one of its aspects. At times it is called an inner instinct; at others, an inner feeling of wholeness. Some speak of deep inner knowledge; others have declared that man, "out of some dark urge, is conscious of the right path." [4] Von Monakow speaks of *hormē* (impulse, driving force), while some, like C. G. Jung, lay stress on archetypal images, recognizing an inner entelechy and thus coming quite close to what medieval philosophy designated as *syneidēsis*, the innermost "focus" and balanced interplay of all natural forces.[5]

The intra-individual dimension shows a typical dual aspect: it is as strongly ego-related as it is value-related. Its ego-relatedness becomes particularly clear when we remember that it is from the depths of the psyche that we receive those alarm signals which register danger, loss, injury, inner discord. Yet from these same depths come feelings of joy and inner satisfaction when the psyche is able to develop naturally. Thus the ego experiences itself either as well balanced, whole and healthy, or as threatened and disunited. The quality of value-relatedness is expressed in the fact that the ego cannot remain indifferent to the voice of the natural disposition but feels itself summoned because it senses value, which it experiences as its own value. This is where obligation and involvement come into play. The intra-individual dimension strives for self-realization, and unless it can accomplish this it is cheated of its meaning and value. On this level, living according to one's conscience simply means letting one's individual potential develop according to its own laws.

4. Goethe, *Faust*, Part I, "Prologue in Heaven."
5. [*Syneidēsis*, amplified in the author's German text as *Zusammenschau*. English: "view together" or "focus."—TRANSLATOR.]

2. The Dimension of Social Commitment and Orientation

We come now to a crucial point. Is it permissible to speak of a social dimension of man's natural disposition, or does everything social belong at the start to the environment? Two things depend on the answer to this question: whether we should condemn all outside influence as a foreign determinant, an artificial interference, and whether we should speak of a "spurious" conscience when social viewpoints are accepted as a criterion. The danger should not be minimized. The personal center is only too often falsified by outside influences, and the individual begins to live by the judgments and expectations of others. Man becomes alienated from himself, and what alone would constitute dignity and truly human behavior soon becomes illusory. The typical mass man lives by the standards of an alien conscience in a state of nonconscience, though usually he is unaware of this because most of his fellow men are exactly like him. For him a "good conscience" simply means conforming with the current moral views. This conception of conscience extends even to the ethics of comradeship found among gangs of criminals. In reality, an alien conscience is not a form of conscience at all but is a counterforce acting against conscience, depersonalizing and deeply dehumanizing man.

Equally uncritical and naïve, however, is the conception which grants conscience complete sovereignty and autonomy, placing the natural disposition in a vacuum, in an autistic, imaginary, solipsistic world of illusions far removed from any concrete reality. Here conscience assumes the role of an autocratic authority, issuing directives and commands without regard to the hierarchy of values in human nature.

The question we must ask, therefore, is a different one: Is human nature not essentially dependent on and oriented toward a social sphere in which alone it can develop naturally? We would misjudge man's nature if we failed to recognize how intimately it is involved and coordinated with the authority of parents and educators as well as with the human community as a whole. Aristotle included the social factor in his

well-known definition of man. For him social commitment and
orientation are constituent elements in man's makeup, and
Catholic philosophy has taken over this view and held it fast.
This is as much as to say that conscience as a natural disposition is partially molded by man's social nature. We know that
the plasticity of man's instincts and aptitudes is greater than in
the animal organism, hence they are more elastic, more varia-
ble, more easily molded. Man is not a self-contained monad; he
is open in all directions. He can realize his best self only as a
member of a community. This is not to deny that an artificial
superego may be constructed if the educational influences are
not consonant with the inner social nature of man but assume
the form of outer coercion masking the educator's self-assertiveness and lust for power. Conscience as a function of man's
whole natural disposition is an expression also of the social
aspect of his nature. Because of that it can warn him against
the worst excesses of the aggressive drive and cruelty which
are given him along with the instinct for self-preservation.

Conscience is not only socially conditioned but also socially
oriented. A very extensive and—in a highly civilized society
—exceedingly costly apparatus of educational influences and
guidance is therefore required for its optimal development. If
we squander the vast sums appropriated for our highly complex educational systems only on the perfecting of technology,
it will be difficult to escape the destructive tendencies of the
atomic age. The dimension of social commitment and orientation which also speaks as the voice of conscience must be
respected.

Today, however, there is a tendency to overemphasize the
social aspect of human nature, which would lead to a cramping
of man's individuality. Disapproval of this trend is expressed in
the papal address mentioned above:

> Protection, respect, love, and service of oneself are not
> only justified but are direct requirements of both psychology
> and moral law. That is at once a self-evident fact of nature
> and an article of Christian faith. The Lord taught: "Thou
> shalt love thy neighbor as thyself" (Mark 12:31). Christ

therefore considered love of oneself to be the criterion of
neighborly love and not the reverse. . . . We should fail to
do justice to this reality if we dismissed all regard for the
ego as psychological imprisonment, as an aberration or a return to a more primitive stage of development, on the pretext
that it is opposed to the natural altruism of the psyche.[6]

The social nature of man is only one of his many dimensions
and must not overshadow any of the others. The voice of
conscience arising from this dimension goes against the true
and natural conscience of the individual unless it rings out in
unison with the other dimensions, and only then should it be
heard and obeyed.

3. The Dimension of Transcendental Relationship

From the center of man's nature, conscience strives for the
fulfillment of all his potentialities, yet at the same time it feels
this process of self-realization as a challenge by a higher authority which man has to recognize. We can therefore understand why he has the impression of being in the presence of
something divine. Is it only a rigid, abstract principle which is
trying to gain recognition, or is it a dynamic, concrete power
through which a divine will issues its summons to man? Ovid
described conscience as *Deus in nobis*, and Seneca called it the
"God who is near you, with you, and in you," adding that "a
holy spirit dwells in us, observing our good and evil." [7]
Whereas it is difficult to conceive that a rigid impersonal
principle—an iron *anankē*—rules over our personal freedom
and dignity, it is relatively easy to accept the idea that the
voice of a personal God speaks directly to us in the dictates of
conscience and that conscience illuminates a third dimension of
human nature: the relation of the image to the prototype.

All this seems fairly unproblematical and self-evident. But
are we really so naïvely uncritical and optimistic in our judg-

---

6. *Acta Apostolica Sedis*, Annus XXXXV, Series II, Vol. XX (1953),
p. 283.
7. [Seneca, Epistle XLI, trans. R. W. Gummere, Loeb Classical Library
edition of Seneca's *Epistulae morales*, Vol. I (Cambridge, Mass., and London, 1917; reprinted 1953).—TRANSLATOR.]

ment of human nature? Or are we—unlike Rousseau—aware of its somber and abysmal aspects, its tendency to fragmentation and ambivalence? The presence of evil is such an elementary fact of human history that we can hardly overlook it. There is that other fascinating voice, likewise resounding from the depths of our being and holding out possibilities of development and self-realization, of richer and lusher experiences far removed from the divine prototype and which, it seems, are likewise deeply embedded in our nature.

Christianity explains this ambivalence by the doctrine of original sin, which has, however, been variously interpreted. According to the Catholic conception, original sin has not in any way inwardly corrupted and poisoned man's nature. The Fall is viewed rather as a breaking-away from friendship with God, resulting in the loss of man's alleged supernatural endowments and in a fatal weakening of his nature as well as a confounding of instinct and spirit. Redemption through Christ must therefore be understood as a summons to man for a resumption of the supernatural filial relationship with God and for the gradual restoration of his weakened nature. According to Catholic doctrine, baptism effectively places Christians within reach of God's love: "We should be called children of God; and so we are" (1 John 3:1, RSV). An actual exaltation and transformation of human nature has been effected, a participation in the divine. But even in this redeemed and blessed nature conscience remains active. It would be inconceivable if only man's biological and sociopsychological nature, and not his exalted nature, should possess in conscience an organ of moral conduct. Through the Holy Spirit, the inner principle of a Christian's life, conscience acquires a new strength, which shall "guide you into all truth" (John 16:8). Conscience is thus the *organon* (tool) of God, "who in a wonderful manner didst create and ennoble human nature, and still more wonderfully hast renewed it," as is said in the Offertory of the Mass.

This increment to our human nature is not forced upon man from outside, by a higher order. He is not urged, still less compelled, by an alien power into a form of behavior fundamentally contrary to the laws of his inner being. Rather, the voice of the spirit strikes a note in accord with the natural spiritual level of the individual and the new level of Christianity he has attained. The extremely difficult and complex problem of the relationship between the natural and the supernatural can only be hinted at in the limited space of this essay.

It takes a considerably deepened theological insight into the church to understand how, for the Catholic, the voice of God can also make itself heard outwardly, through the teaching office. For the Catholic, the church is not just an external organization, like a club you can join or leave at will. It is the outward and visible expression of that invisible community which, as the *corpus Christi mysticum*, embraces all those who have received the new life. It is obvious that this new, living community also entails new forms, new laws, and a new kind of freedom as well as new obligations. Conscience thus acquires a new function. Both the intra-individual and the social dimension of *syneidēsis* are deepened and expanded by the transcendental dimension. Through his participation in the divine, man enters into communion with the *corpus Christi mysticum*. While the church should not be identified with Christ in all its organizational forms and institutions, it should not be understood either as separate from Christ, its central life-giving principle. Furthermore, we should have to reject as altogether too primitive any attempt to explain the difference between Catholicism and Protestantism simply by contrasting the church and Christ. The antithesis "Catholics are church-bound whereas Protestants affirm that salvation can be found only in Christ," or "Catholics remain dependent on the authority of the church whereas Protestants recognize in Christ alone the direct road to God," does not show even a superficial understanding of Catholic theology. The way in which the early church bore witness to the social dimension of Christian conscience is too overwhelming to be passed over in silence.

None other than Paul himself took great pains to indoctrinate the Christians of his time with this new concept. As a former Pharisee, he was well aware of the practical importance and sublime grandeur of moral law, and his conversion to the new morality of Christian freedom was an experience that cut to the core of his being. Nowhere do we encounter a more soul-stirring debate than in his Epistle to the Galatians, which is the greatest proclamation of freedom in Christianity. The sentences ring out like a fanfare of trumpets: "Stand fast therefore in the liberty wherewith Christ hath made us free, and be not entangled again with the yoke of bondage" (5:1). "For, brethren, ye have been called unto liberty" (5:13). And then, when the epoch-making articles of liberation stood there as if hewn in rock, he himself came to experience the paradox of Christian conscience: the new, overwhelming freedom of conscience turned out to be a yet mightier bondage to this same conscience. The highest and truest criterion of the Christian attitude had to be hammered out in the debate with Gnostic ideology, and here the bond of love proved more decisive and more powerful than freedom. The most important passages can be found in 1 Corinthians, chapters 8–13. Paul's thinking circles in spirals around the central problem of freedom and bondage. Actually, he says, the Christian is free to eat of "those things that are offered in sacrifice unto idols" (8:4); actually, in Christ, woman has equal rights with man (11:11–12); actually, all gifts of the spirit are important and great (chap. 12). *But* Christianity has to employ a wholly different and new criterion, a new norm of conscience: the norm and criterion of love (chap. 13). This love is so far-reaching that a man will surrender his freedom if it happens to be harmful to a fellow Christian who lacks the courage and inner freedom of the stronger one. The Christian conscience grants freedom but it also binds anew through that freely expressed love for the community of those sharing the new life wrought in the depths of their being by the Holy Spirit (12:12–14, 25–28).

THREE DIMENSIONS are thus conferred on us by *syneidēsis:* the intra-individual, the social, and the transcendental, which interpenetrate and complement one another. *Syneidēsis* might be considered as a function of that image of man which dwells deep in the psyche and strives for progressive development and realization. But this image is seldom seen whole and complete in any given age. Each period tends to stress new or hitherto neglected aspects, while previous ones are pushed aside with equal bias. Thus every epoch is called upon to acquire an ever more comprehensive and penetrating knowledge of human nature. Today we may acknowledge with particular gratitude the findings of anthropological psychology since they afford us a more refined and effective understanding of *syneidēsis* and its significance for our time. The disposition for conscience will, of course, always be fundamental in all decisions which are of universal importance to human life. Its peculiar dynamism will always assert itself, provided that the somatic, psychological, and spiritual functions are relatively sound, that the social organism is reasonably well ordered, and that the individual does not deliberately cut himself off from the gift of Christian grace. In other words, conscience is not a free-floating entity but rests on a normative and natural foundation.

The stage is thus set on which the drama of decision by conscience is enacted. We have established the point of departure from which the conscience of the Catholic summons him to responsible and ethical action. To *syneidēsis* we might apply the oracle: *Vocatus atque non vocatus, deus aderit* ("summoned or not summoned, God will be present").[8] It is the immanent God who abides within us and summons us, the God whose image awaits realization in the depths of the psyche: "Let us make man in our image, after our likeness" (Gen. 1:26). For concrete application in life, the practical judgments and verdicts of conscience must be formed on the foundation of *syneidēsis*.

8. [Delphic oracle given to the Lacedaemonians when they asked whether they should make war against the Athenians. The oracle is carved over the front door of C. G. Jung's house in Küsnacht.—TRANSLATOR.]

II. Conscience as an Act of Free Decision

Although conscience, as integral to the structure of our human nature, presents itself to us as a binding and determining factor, the authentic act of conscience is the result of a wholly free and personal decision. This state of affairs sounds relatively simple, but it is very difficult to describe more precisely, because here we touch on the mystery of human freedom. The mystery resides in the fact that human freedom can never be absolute. It must continually reconstitute and realize itself anew because of the multiplicity of determinisms which are at work in nature. To begin with, it can be established that authentic and well-considered judgments of conscience are not very common. In many situations of life, *syneidēsis* as the foundation of judgments of conscience functions almost automatically, so that it is relatively easy for a man to act in accordance with his natural disposition. But, in the life of every human being, situations arise and decisions must be made which confront him with more complex problems. The different dimensions of *syneidēsis* then seem to conflict with one another, and careful reflection is required before conscience can exercise judgment and arrive at a straightforward decision. There are people who are faced again and again with such decisions, indeed their whole life seems to consist of endless decision-making. Others, more matter of fact and more integrated, allow themselves to be guided quietly and surely by their natural disposition. People who are burdened with problems, who are less integrated, are more intensely aware of the divergent possibilities, the dissonances, the polarities of their being and for this reason must make conscious decisions more frequently. They continually experience conscience in its executive function, as taking up a personal position, as an act of spiritual freedom.

In order to demonstrate the full significance of the act of decision, we shall discuss it under three headings which are especially important from the Catholic point of view: (1) the

act of free decision proper, (2) the right of the erring conscience, and (3) the church and freedom of conscience.

1. The Act of Free Decision Proper

Correctly understood, this act is carried out in three phases.
The first and the third are well known, while the second seems
to elude phenomenological description.

Catholic moralists have described the first phase as *conscientia antecedens* (antecedent conscience). In this phase conscience again appears as a natural disposition, but this time
before the forum of intellectual reflection, stating its case in
the form of a practical judgment and demanding attention.
The cogent arguments for or against a particular mode of
conduct are there deliberated. In this phase the appellant hears
the voice that warns him against evading the issue or admonishes him not to repress *syneidēsis,* while at the same time
encouraging him to act correctly.

In the third phase, *conscientia consequens* (subsequent conscience) raises its voice as the incorruptible prosecutor, if a
mistake has been committed, or as the corroborative witness of
right behavior and action. Remorse or peace of mind are the
outcome of this phase. In both these phases man experiences an
inner tension—perhaps a disturbing gap or even a conflict—
between his ego and the dictates of conscience. Conscience
appears here clearly as a nonego, as a higher self.

Between these two phases lies the second phase, where conscience makes the decision proper. This decision seems to be
carried out by the innermost psychic center, which pronounces judgment in full freedom and accepts the responsibility. In this act the ego experiences the potential identity of
conscience with the self or else its own infinite detachment
from it. The Schoolmen were much given to elaborate and
deep speculation about this act, and each school of thought
evolved different theories concerning the psychic function
that makes the decision. Albertus Magnus and Thomas Aquinas defended the intellectualistic, and Alexander of Hales,
Bonaventure, and Henry of Ghent the voluntaristic theory.

Nowadays we are inclined to accept the so-called holistic theory, which postulates the interplay of all psychic faculties in this act. Here we come face to face with the mystery of the individual; here he experiences his highest and strongest potentialities, but also his inalienable personal responsibility. The act of decision cannot be performed in an atmosphere of willful, arbitrary, or frivolous freedom. It requires the utmost seriousness of purpose.

It is on this freedom that morality of action is founded. Through it the objective demands of man as a microcosm, an image of totality, are subjectivized and recast into a personal confession of faith—or are rejected and excluded from this innermost sphere.

In this realm of personal freedom there are no longer any determining influences from outside. Here even the Catholic has to make the judgments of conscience entirely by himself, and in this respect his position is in no way different from that of the Protestant or the true humanist, unbeliever though he may be. The Catholic has to follow the judgment of conscience even if, objectively speaking, it is erroneous, and even if it should separate him from his church. The judgment of conscience is absolutely binding: it commits man to himself and to God. No excuses and no appeals to the commands of military or ecclesiastical authorities are of avail here. There is no replacement or substitute for personal conscience. Authority is valid only to the extent that it can justify itself as competent and binding before the bar of a mature and serene conscience.

Man cannot abstain from these judgments since they are not subjective, arbitrary opinions or expressions of momentary experiences but grow out of the inner bond with *syneidēsis*, thus indirectly revealing God's will. Subjective caprice can give in, conform, or bow to totalitarian pressure any time it seems opportune to do so. But conscience can win the struggle for freedom in the face of all the arbitrary demands of human institutions precisely because it is bound by the true and unconditional demands of nature herself.

Are we now affirming, after all, that conscience is *absolutely* autonomous and sovereign? By no means. Our discussion of *syneidēsis* has shown how closely conscience is tied to the objective order of its own multifaceted nature. Within the many dimensions of this moral order, wherein is expressed the will of God the creator and redeemer, there is no freedom of conscience. The freedom that remains to it consists in its opening itself to demands that are in accord with its highest nature and in striving, by this inner assent, to do them justice. Only in this sense is the phrase "freedom of conscience" meaningful and attuned to the nature and dignity of man. And this is also the position we must adopt in elucidating the seeming contradictions in the attitude of the church and its official pronouncements.

2. The Right of the Erring Conscience

Conscience would be an effective guarantor of moral order if we could assume that its decisions and judgments were ordinarily based on *syneidēsis* and were followed by actions not subject to outside interference. The sole reason for the failure of conscience would then lie in the second phase of the act of free decision. Freedom to decide would carry the entire responsibility for any deviations and for all behavior running counter to *syneidēsis*. We would then be entitled to a certain amount of optimism regarding the morality of individual conduct and of society at large. But world history, as well as the public and private lives of individuals, has taught us a different lesson: injustices great and small, intrigues, egotism and self-assertiveness, brutal jockeying for position, and downright criminality cannot be considered rare exceptions. Are they indicative of a blatant failure of the freedom of conscience? Are injustice and evil always only the product of a free decision against the better knowledge of *conscientia?* Or is it conceivable that logical and, perhaps more often, emotionally conditioned errors have already crept in at the very moment when conscience forms its judgment? As a matter of fact, dynamic psychology is engaged in investigating the gradual evolution of psychic modes of behavior, and it attempts to explain the formation of emotionally or intellectually conditioned attitudes and judgments in terms of educational influences, collective opinions, and individual moral prejudices. *Syneidēsis* does indeed provide the ground plan and the most elementary, primary requirements for a truly human existence. But in the derivation of secondary ethical standards conflicts between two or more basic principles may arise, leading to erroneous conclusions or furnishing pretexts for falsifications based on affect. Errors may then not only seem permissible but may even appear as dictates of conscience, although deeper insight and more careful, disinterested consideration and judgment would show them to be contrary to the moral order. There is, evidently, an erring conscience, and we must ask ourselves whether such a conscience should be entitled to the same freedom as an incorruptible conscience which much practical experience has rendered capable of great objectivity of judgment.

Are the head-hunters of Borneo entitled to their trophies and to this grisly ritual which promises them increased magical powers? Should the burning of widows in India be considered the legitimate right of a free conscience, since it gives expression to a lofty conception of marital union? And is temple prostitution in India acceptable because it is practiced in the name of the god of fertility? Are we compelled to acknowledge the right of communism to exist and to spread propaganda, knowing as we do that it undermines the foundations of true democracy and works systematically for its overthrow? Can conscience absolve people who refuse to pay taxes because of their conviction that the money would be squandered by the government anyway?

To formulate the question theoretically, are all convictions based on conscience *equally* entitled to freedom because each is the expression of personal conscience, even though they may be contrary to the generally accepted convictions of the day? The topicality of this question is felt again and again, as when we learn that the Skoptsy, a Russian religious sect, practice self-mutilation and that the Chlystes, another Russian sect, indulge in sexual orgies as part of their ritual; that, in 1948, the Oldenburg police were barely able to prevent the human sacrifice of two refugee children from eastern Europe by members of a nonstop prayer group who sought in this manner to forestall the imminent end of the world; and that, in 1954, members of a religious sect in Marseilles allowed their children to die because its teachings forbade them to call a doctor.

The question of divergent opinions in the matter of an objective moral order or the possibility of recognizing objective, ultimate, and absolute truths is not peculiar to our time. Thomas Aquinas was familiar with it in another form and gave his own answer: "Belief in Christ is good in itself and necessary for salvation. But if a Christian who held it wrong to believe in Christ were to do so, he would commit a sin." [9]

Thus the right of the erring conscience was recognized in the Catholic Middle Ages too. Those who err innocently, having acted according to their best knowledge and conscience, cannot be morally condemned even if they have acted immorally according to the general consensus. Whether or not they should be punished nonetheless is another question altogether. A delinquent acting from conviction may be able to justify himself before his own conscience, but the state has to consider the welfare of society as a whole. It must defend law and order by making the delinquent aware of the fact that his conscience is at odds with the existing order.

We might go a step further and declare that those who commit an error of conscience should not be forced to act against their conscience. It is their moral right not to be obliged to act contrary to their conscience even if it is in error. Thus a conscientious objector may be employed in some civilian occupation, and one may try to persuade him that he is acting in error, but on no account should he be forced to take up arms if he considers it to be a sin against his conscience.

On the other hand, we believe there is an essential difference

9. *Summa Theologica*, I/II, 19.5.

between not having the right to force people into certain actions against their conscience and actually giving them the right to live publicly by the convictions of their conscience if this would violate the rights of others. Anyone preparing and promoting the overthrow of the existing order may, of course, justify himself in the name of his convictions, but we cannot oblige the representatives of that order to allow these convictions to take positive effect. While he is thus prevented from carrying out his presumed duty to his conscience, he is not required to violate it. Duty to one's conscience ceases, however, when it becomes impossible to carry it out. The erring conscience as such remains inviolate, but its consequences may be prevented.

3. The Church and Freedom of Conscience

For the Catholic, conscience is the supreme authority even in matters relating to his faith and his membership in the Catholic church. The pronouncement of Lactantius in the third century against the Roman law enforcing religious sacrifice should never be forgotten: "Nisi enim sponte et ex animo fiat, execratio est" ("Unless the act is done freely and from the heart, it is an abomination accursed").[10] In the same spirit, Thomas Aquinas teaches that "anyone upon whom the ecclesiastical authorities, in ignorance of the true facts, impose a demand that offends against his clear conscience, should perish in excommunication rather than violate his conscience."[11] The doctrine and the fundamental attitude of the church are thus quite unequivocal and cannot give rise to any doubts.

On the other hand, we cannot deny the facts of history. The Inquisition, which became in effect an institution for the mass violation of conscience, and individual cases, of which Galileo's is only the best known, are no light mortgage for a church that considers itself the advocate of human dignity. For centuries the church had to fight for its own freedom of conscience.

10. Lactantius *Divinarum Institutionum* V. 19 [*Patr. Lat.* (Migne), VI. 20. 614–16].
11. IV, *Sent., dist.* 38, art. 4, expos. text.

To this day the names of those witnesses who paid for it with
their lives are recorded in the church martyrology and are
continually being recited. It is indeed inconceivable how the
church was able to change its attitude so quickly—not in
doctrine but in practice. We cannot and do not wish to defend
this *volte face*. Today it is possible to say this in public and to
write about it. Albert Hartmann, a Jesuit, exposed the facts as
follows in his book *Toleranz und christlicher Glaube:* "By
means of bloody martyrdom the church fought for the freedom of conscience against the pagan state, until it was proclaimed for the first time in the historic Edict of Tolerance at
Milan in 311. But later this same church denied others that
freedom and persecuted people for the sake of their faith." [12]
Only the honest admission of past errors can offer some slight
guarantee against easy repetition of similar abuses of power in
the future. Justice demands, however, that in judging the
church we should consider as extenuating circumstances the
conditions of the time, such as the absence of psychological
insight and the close ties of the church with the existing social
and political order.

Nevertheless, certain doctrinal statements made by the
church in the nineteenth century, though apparently directed
against the freedom of conscience, must be viewed in a different light. It is easy to misconstrue them. In 1832 Gregory XVI
condemned as "absurd and erroneous and even as *deliramen-
tum*"—folly—the idea that "freedom of conscience should be
proclaimed and secured for all." [13] In 1864 Pius IX took
Gregory's statement as a precedent and confirmed it. [14] The
freedom of conscience attacked here is that arbitrary freedom
which recognizes none of the binding values of truth and the
moral order. Its advocates ignore the foundations of conscience in human nature in order to defend the sovereignty and

12. Albert Hartmann, *Toleranz und christlicher Glaube* (Frankfurt
a.M., 1955), p. 172.
13. *Mirari Vos* (1832) (Sammlung Marmy, 1945, No. 16). [See *Papal
Teachings* (Boston: Daughters of St. Paul, 1962), pp. 124 ff.—EDITOR.]
14. *Quanta Cura* (1864).

autonomy necessary to them for making decisions as and when
they please. Gregory's words were directed against the idea
that anyone may consider right what seems to him so at any
given moment and without paying his due to the standards set
by nature and divine revelation. Freedom of conscience must
not become a *carte blanche* for a specious, worldly morality.

But, is there not after all a coercive aspect of dogma, compelling the Catholic to adhere to the tenets of the faith which
are proclaimed as universally binding revealed truths? For
many people this is the greatest stumbling block as far as their
attitude to the church is concerned. Where, then, is there any
room for freedom of conscience? Within the space of this
essay it would be quite impossible to make anything like an
exhaustive study of these problems, which raise so many difficult questions. We can only hint at an answer, without sub-
stantiating it in detail.

The Catholic church believes that in the exercise of its
infallible teaching office it has the support of the Holy Scriptures. It insists that it was founded by Christ himself, together
with the institution of this teaching office and also its pastoral
function. "He that heareth you heareth me" (Luke 10:16). It
insists equally on the institution of primacy in the church:
"Thou art Peter, and upon this rock I will build my church"
(Matt. 16:18). We know, of course, that outside the Catholic
church these texts have been interpreted differently and that in
the past two centuries new interpretations have been continually put forward which are in part diametrically opposed to
the Catholic one. Which of these interpretations is the correct
one to which Christians can look for guidance? Does the level
of exegetical knowledge at a given time determine what constitutes the body of faith for the Christian, or can he choose from
among the many different viewpoints the one that seems most
plausible to him? Or should he follow the zigzag path of
continually changing interpretations? We are in no way blind
to the fact that in individual cases the coercive aspect of dogma
may lead to very serious spiritual conflicts. This is particularly
true, for instance, when an eminent theologian has doubts

about the conclusiveness of a certain dogma or even feels that he must reject it altogether.

We are fully aware of the tremendous significance which the mere existence of an infallible teaching office has. Although the formal assent of faith is required only for tenets solemnly pronounced *ex cathedra*, in many other matters of faith and morals decisions which are not solemnly pronounced are also relatively binding. It would be unrealistic and dishonest not to admit that very often this is the crucial point which determines whether the Catholic will profess his allegiance to the church's view or whether he will hold it incompatible with his personal freedom of conscience. But very often this is also the point at which considerable confusion arises, because some Catholics make adherence to the dogma and moral teachings of the church responsible for their own lack of spiritual freedom, for their neurotic inhibitions and frustrations. Closer examination of these neurotic symptoms and careful analysis of the psychic background shows, however, that in most cases the lack of spiritual freedom is due rather to an overstrict and harsh upbringing or to a false understanding of the church's precepts. We are in entire agreement with John B. Hirschmann, a Jesuit, when he writes: "We should neither deny nor minimize nor peremptorily dismiss the impression which some, perhaps too many, of its members have today of a certain lack of freedom within the church." [15] But we should do well to make a clear distinction between lack of spiritual freedom and spiritual commitment. Too often lack of spiritual freedom is caused by spiritual confusion and lack of insight into the coherence of Catholic doctrine. The spirit is oriented toward and committed to truth. Noncommitment does not make free, but truth which is assimilated to reality does. The reality principle so much emphasized by depth psychology is all-embracing and has universal validity. We are not the creators of reality. We must learn to recognize and accept it as completely as possible, even

15. "Die Freiheit in der Kirche," *Stimmen der Zeit* (1957/58), Heft 2, p. 86.

when we meet it as spiritual and supernatural reality. Both the teaching and pastoral offices of the church serve this great reality and thereby the truth which makes free the children of God. This is why the church was promised the Paraclete, "the Spirit of truth" (John 16:13). Through him the competence and scope of this service are firmly established, but also its limitations, because only voluntary obedience, and not the outward performance of duty, constitutes a moral achievement for free and emancipated human beings.

For this reason it is very important that no one should ever be forced into this faith and into membership in the church. Canon 1351 of the Canon Law puts it succinctly: "No one may be forced to accept the Catholic faith against his will." In 1943 and again in 1946 Pius XII quoted this canon, adding: "For faith, without which it is impossible to please God, must be an entirely free homage of the intellect and will. Hence, if it should happen that, contrary to the constant teaching of this Apostolic See, anyone should be brought against his will to embrace the Catholic faith, we cannot do otherwise, in the realization of our duty, than disavow such an action." [16]

On this basis the personal freedom of the act of decision is ensured and the personal responsibility of conscience recognized. Hence even for Catholics conscience is the ultimate authority from which there can be no appeal to a higher one. Here again there is a broad consensus, at least among civilized peoples.

In the light of these considerations we can understand why the Catholic church is so vitally interested in the education of conscience. It cannot remain indifferent, since it regards not only the teaching office but also the pastoral office as its allotted task. Obviously, this task is of such magnitude and reaches so far into all realms of life that it would be necessary to devote an entire essay to this topic alone. The education of

16. *Mystici corporis* (1943) (Sammlung Marmy, No. 1441). [See *The Documents of Vatican II*, ed. Walter M. Abbott (New York: America Press, Association Press, 1966), p. 689; see also *Acta Apostolica Sedis*, No. 38 (1946), p. 394.—EDITOR.]

conscience is probably the most difficult task all educators have to face, and it is one that continually presents itself in new form. We are fully aware of the extent to which the Catholic education of conscience again and again falls short of what it should accomplish, and how great—and almost inevitable—is this failure.

While we may have succeeded in sketching a Catholic view of conscience in broad outline, most of the ideas touched on here would have to be studied in much greater depth in order to do it full justice. Conscience is the focal point on which all problems concerning the image of man and of God, the individual and the collective, the subjectivity and objectivity of our knowledge, converge. This shows with particular clarity that conscience is the battleground where our spiritual forces must carry out their true struggle for decisions.

Freud and Conscience

Ernst Blum

Translated by R. F. C. Hull

If psycho-analysis has not hitherto shown its appreciation of certain things, this has never been because it overlooked their achievement or sought to deny their importance, but because it followed a particular path, which had not yet led so far. And finally, when it had reached them, things have a different look to it from what they have to others.[1]

ALL OF US have certainly had the experience that it is not the extraordinary things of life that hold the greatest secrets but the everyday things. Everything that we have to do with every day, that we continually experience, becomes banal and self-evident, and we no longer see the secrets which are woven into the fabric of life. It is in this manner that we also treat conscience; we treat it, in fact, as if it were a broom or a vacuum cleaner, which annoys us if it does not stand in its accustomed place or does not function. We speak airily of our good or our bad conscience, but we dismiss it with the greatest of ease, shoving it into a corner when we are not actually using it but demanding that it shall function properly whenever we find it necessary.

And yet it is something crucial: we all know about conscience and know that we have a conscience whether we will or not. In times of trouble and distress we "feel" it more, for better or worse; and when we are despairingly thrown back on our own resources, then only do we begin to come to grips with it. It is then that the elect, the holy men and saints of

1. Sigmund Freud, Preface to "The Ego and the Id" (1923), *The Complete Psychological Works of Sigmund Freud*, Vol. XIX, p. 12. [All references to Freud's works will be to this Standard Edition (hereafter cited as "S.E."), translated under the general editorship of James Strachey, in collaboration with Anna Freud, assisted by Alix Strachey and Alan Tyson; published by The Macmillan Company, New York and London, 1953——.]

religion or the great minds of philosophy, experience to the full the anguish of what we call conscience. We have all heard of their struggles.

What the investigator of the psyche has to say, when stripped of the trappings of feeling and rhetoric, sounds positively sober by comparison, almost as if, instead of conducting a symphony, one were only expounding the theory of composition. This disappointment I can spare no one. Let us remember, however, that though one cannot create a symphony from the theory of composition alone, one can create a theory of composition from the symphony. It needs the genius of the composer to reveal the laws of his work to us—laws that are held to be sacred—and not the principles of mathematics and physics.

It is in this way that Sigmund Freud came up against the problem of conscience. It was not the zeal of the investigator alone that made him the creator of psychoanalysis, but first and foremost his encounter with human suffering. There he found all human suffering is the *suffering of conscience*. It was this discovery that impelled him to forge the instrument of psychoanalysis, with which he tried to bring the sufferer release or at least alleviation from his pains. Though forged from a knowledge of human suffering, it became at the same time a means of knowledge. Thus, by reciprocal action, instrument and knowledge developed concurrently, each promoting the growth of the other.

I can see my reader shaking his head doubtfully over my assertion that it was the pangs of his patients' consciences that led Freud to psychoanalysis. Freud's doctrine, he will say, enjoys the repute, or rather disrepute, of wanting to know nothing of conscience, man's so-called better part, and has little or no use for it. Not to mince matters, it was, on the contrary, the sexual suffering of man that Freud regarded as the root of all evil. Here I must plead with all my readers to abandon their preconceived opinions. They should remember that suffering is not simply measured by the painfulness of a condition, as though it were a weight. Even a weight becomes a problem for us only if we have to lift or carry it, and it can become suffering if our strength fails or gives out. Suffering, therefore, is not a static condition but a conflict, a struggle between two forces, whether between our inner forces and an external power or between two forces within ourselves. When we talk of sexual suffering, we mean, in the strictest as well as in the broadest sense, nothing else than the struggle between our passions and our conscience.

So there it is again—conscience. For conscience is not anything static, either. It directs itself *to* something in us, *against* something, and we have constantly to direct ourselves in relation to our conscience. It exercises a *directing* function and causes us to orient ourselves to something. It is in this sense that Freud himself described conscience as our "inner judge and director" (*Richter*) and as an agency that gives our impulses "direction" (*Richtung*) toward what we hold to be "right" (*richtig, Recht*). But with this train of thought we have sped far ahead of our task. We must now retrace our steps and try to take up our position anew.

I have been asked what Freud's psychoanalysis has to say about the problem of conscience. Let us broaden the question: Can psychology say anything at all about this problem, in general terms? Is conscience one of the psychological "categories"? These questions are unanswerable, for up to the present no one has succeeded in delineating, categorically, the position of psychology within a scientific system. That is why Freud, whenever he concerned himself with conscience—and he did so from his first work to his last—approached it very gingerly as a concept, considering it to be something probably belonging to man a priori but not regarding it as any kind of given psychological knowledge. He expressed himself thoughtfully even when conscience began to open itself to psychoanalytic insight: "I might simply say that the special agency which I am beginning to distinguish in the ego is conscience. But it is more prudent to keep the agency as something independent and to suppose that conscience is one of its functions." ² Elsewhere he says: "If such an agency does exist, we cannot possibly come upon it as a *discovery*—we can only *recognize* it." ³

If, from the beginning to the end of our exposition, we have to break through the framework of a purely psychoanalytic presentation, this is not due to a play of ideas but springs rather from an inner necessity. To follow Freud's thought processes, we have to proceed in two directions: the biological, on the one hand, and the anthropological and existential, on the other. For—in my personal opinion at least—psychoanalysis is situated between the two, and it passes over into both without limit.

So far as the biological approach is concerned, I will leave the floor to my revered teacher and master, Constantin von Monakow, whose intellectual work goes far beyond the bounds of neurology and brain research. For him, life, whose biological driving force he calls *hormē*, is from the beginning endowed with the "striving for perfection, for the building-up of relations with other organisms, with the environment, and, beyond that, with the universe." ⁴ Thus the "primordial feeling" he ascribes to *hormē* is already religiously oriented. The instincts, "as a propulsive force continually emanating from *hormē*," do not embrace only the instinct of self-preservation and the sexual instinct. Monakow also assumes a social and religious instinct as "a prime biological datum," on the evidence that "among the phenomena of life there are some of a special kind which, through the nature of their effects and their prospective tendency, extend beyond the individual as observed at a given moment into the infinity of space, time, and the universe." The harmony or, in biological terms, the regulation of this system is guaranteed by a "principle of self-regulation of the functions," which he calls *syneidēsis* and

2. *New Introductory Lectures on Psycho-Analysis* (1933), S.E. XXII, 60.
3. "On Narcissism: An Introduction" (1914), S.E. XIV, 95.
4. Constantin von Monakow, *Gehirn und Gewissen* (Zurich: Morgarten-Verlag Conzett & Huber, 1950), p. 65. The next few quotations are from pages 74-75 of this work.

which is nothing other than biological conscience. Monakow explains how this *syneidēsis* "progresses through various unconscious and conscious stages in child and adult to moral and religious conscience," how it has to come to grips with suggestion and mass suggestion, with individual passions (an "expression of the tempestuous proliferation of a particular instinct"), and with vices (criminality), and how its activity can be demonstrated in all manifestations of life as well as in the "insults" to the world of instinct (neurosis, psychosis, whether individual or collective). In his passage through life the "giant protoplasm Man," [5] from the smallest bodily process to his highest spiritual achievement, stands under the jurisdiction of a "directory," an "optimal order of functions and life tasks," a biological conscience which is finally reflected "in his consciousness as *human* conscience," as the "*civilized human will*." [6] This conscience not only acts for the future interests of man and humanity; it also, as Monakow says, *summons* man to *responsibility*. [7]

Thus far the biologist. Let us now leave the floor to my second teacher and master, Sigmund Freud. What he has in common with Monakow is the idea that life is guided by the instincts, whose interplay is guaranteed by a principle grown out of the world of instinct through the process of ego-formation, the superego, which ultimately becomes the vehicle of the stirrings of conscience.

But whereas Monakow emphasizes the harmonious operation of *hormē* and *syneidēsis*, Freud is far more impressed by the dichotomy in man and the antinomies of existence. Man struggles constantly for harmony, and this struggle is born of the natural and necessary counterplay of Eros and Thanatos. Destruction and aggression are a principle as primary as Eros, not simply something negative; from this "power that continually denies" (*Faust*) there springs, in necessary and ultimately harmonious alliance with Eros, the "good deed," and culture,

5. *Ibid.*, p. 231.
6. *Ibid.*, p. 240.
7. *Ibid.*, p. 248.

civilization, society, and human fellowship flourish. More and more of the egoistic strivings are transformed by erotic affluxes into altruistic, social ones. "The development of the individual seems to us to be a product of the interaction between two urges, the urge towards happiness, which we call 'egoistic,' and the urge towards union with others in the community, which we call 'altruistic.' . . . Here by far the most important thing is the aim of creating a unity out of the individual human beings." [8] To reach this goal, "civilization has to use its utmost efforts in order to set limits to man's aggressive instincts and to hold the manifestations of them in check by psychical reaction-formations." [9] The means employed for this purpose is introjection, the interiorization of aggressiveness. "There it is taken over by a portion of the ego, which sets itself over against the rest of the ego as super-ego, and which now, in the form of 'conscience,' is ready to put into action against the ego the same harsh aggressiveness that the ego would have liked to satisfy upon other, extraneous individuals." [10] Thus aggressiveness is turned by the superego into the authoritarian dictate of conscience.

In one of his first works [11] Freud had recognized that the inner conflict leading to psychic illness was a failure of defense against incompatible ideas. Patients of this class

> had enjoyed good mental health up to the moment at which *an occurrence of incompatibility took place in their ideational life*—that is to say, until their ego was faced with an experi-ence, an idea or a feeling which aroused such a distressing affect that the subject decided to forget about it because he had no confidence in his power to resolve the contradictions between that incompatible idea and his ego by means of thought-activity.[12]

By means of this defense, regarded at that time also as "repression," "the ego succeeds in freeing itself from the con-

8. *Civilization and Its Discontents* (1930), S.E. XXI, 140.
9. *Ibid.*, p. 112.
10. *Ibid.*, p. 123.
11. "The Neuro-Psychoses of Defence" (1894), S.E. III.
12. *Ibid.*, p. 47.

tradictions; but instead, it has burdened itself with a mnemonic symbol which finds a lodgement in consciousness, like a sort of parasite . . . and which persists there until a conversion in the opposite direction takes place." [13] The patient suffers from an unbearable sense of guilt, arising from the feeling of the failure of his struggle against the ideas and impulses he has rejected. What is revealed here is nothing less than a conflict of conscience, and the ideas and impulses are unendurable precisely because they are not compatible with conscience. Consequently the ego, or some agency in it, tries to dismiss them from consciousness, to repress them.[14] There is thus a repressing agency, a moral valuer. Psychic illness proves to be the failure to solve a conflict this agency has caused.

Before long Freud speaks also of the pangs of conscience felt by obsessional patients and connects them with the sense of guilt. "We may say that the sufferer from compulsions and prohibitions behaves as if he were dominated by a sense of guilt, of which, however, he knows nothing, so we must call it an unconscious sense of guilt, in spite of the apparent contradiction in terms." [15] Just as devout believers, confessing that they are "miserable sinners at heart," offer up their prayers and invocations, the sense of guilt forces the man who does *not* confess his trespasses, and *because* he does not confess them takes no responsibility for them, into his illness. We shall have more to say about the origin of these guilt feelings and their relation to the judicial agency.

We get a closer glimpse of Freud's insightful observations in his book *Totem and Taboo*.[16] The meaning of "taboo" is well known. It is a Polynesian word signifying on the one hand "holy, hallowed," and on the other "eerie, dangerous, unclean." "Our collocation 'holy dread' would often coincide in meaning with 'taboo.' " [17]

13. *Ibid.*, p. 49.
14. "Further Remarks on the Neuro-Psychoses of Defence" (1896), S.E. III.
15. "Obsessive Actions and Religious Practices" (1907), S.E. IX, 123.
16. *Totem and Taboo* (1912–13), S.E. XIII.
17. *Ibid.*, p. 18.

"If I am not mistaken," says Freud,

> the explanation of taboo also throws light on the nature and origin of *conscience*. It is possible, without any stretching of the sense of the term, to speak of a taboo conscience or, after a taboo has been violated, of a taboo sense of guilt. Taboo conscience is probably the earliest form in which the phenomenon of conscience is met with.
>
> For what is "conscience"? On the evidence of language it is related to that of which one is "most certainly conscious." Indeed, in some languages the words for "conscience" and "consciousness" can scarcely be distinguished.
>
> Conscience is the internal perception of the rejection of a particular wish operating within us. The stress, however, is upon the fact that this rejection has no need to appeal to anything else for support, that it is quite certain of itself. This is even clearer in the case of consciousness of guilt—the perception of the internal condemnation of an act by which we have carried out a particular wish. To put forward any reason for this would seem superfluous: anyone who has a conscience must feel within him the justification for the condemnation, must feel the self-reproach for the act that has been carried out. This same characteristic is to be seen in the savage's attitude towards taboo. It is a command issued by conscience; any violation of it produces a fearful sense of guilt which follows as a matter of course and of which the origin is unknown.[18]

Without going more closely into the connections between this sacrosanct taboo conscience and the psychic nature and magical world of those primitive peoples who are dominated by it, we may yet be impressed by the similarities of structure and effect which that "collective conscience" has with our individual conscience. Above all, we recognize the indissoluble unity of the sense of guilt and the conscience-producing agency.

These taboo regulations can now reveal to us the inner impulses against which they are directed and which merit condemnation. Not only psychoanalysis but research in depth psychology as well as ethnopsychology has been able to estab-

18. *Ibid.*, pp. 67 f.

lish the existence of instinctual impulses and wishes deeply rooted in man's unconscious which originally aimed at parricide and incest. Both these belong to the primal motifs of humanity. Myths, legends, religions, rites, legal institutions, feast days and festivals, as well as the subterranean impulses of individuals, all bear witness to these fateful primordial processes in our unconscious. We shall leave aside the question of whether the motifs of parricide and incest have their roots in an even more aboriginal, archaic stock of ideas, as is persuasively argued by Jung and his school (Neumann and others). In any case, parricide and incest can be shown to be guilt motifs, and they also underlie the processes which Freud highlighted as the Oedipus complex in the fate of the individual.

In general we can say, or rather Freud says:

> There can be no doubt that the Oedipus complex may be looked upon as one of the most important sources of the sense of guilt by which neurotics are so often tormented. But more than this: in a study of the beginnings of human religion and morality which I published in 1913 under the title of *Totem and Taboo* I put forward a suggestion that mankind as a whole may have acquired its sense of guilt, the ultimate source of religion and morality, at the beginning of its history, in connection with the Oedipus complex.[19]

I feel obliged to say something more about these first object-relationships which are enacted in the Oedipus complex, and especially about their effects on the formation of conscience. Although myths, legends, folk customs, and religion offer abundant proof that the first object-relationships between child and parent are particularly fateful, as we have already seen in the case of taboo regulations, it remained for Freud and Jung to demonstrate to us that these impulses and processes still play a role in the psychic life of the individual today. Very early on, discordant impulses become manifest in the emotional attitudes of the child to the parents. The child's love and hostility lead to a real conflict between the generations, in

---

19. *Introductory Lectures on Psycho-Analysis* (1916–17), Part III, S.E. XVI, 331 f.

which, *among other things,* love for the parent of the opposite sex and hate for the parent of the same sex are played out as an inner struggle in the form of a dichotomy. Borrowing from the Oedipus myth, which has all the compelling force of destiny, Freud named these processes the Oedipus complex. The destiny of Oedipus

> moves us only because it might have been ours—because the oracle laid the same curse upon us before our birth as upon him. It is the fate of all of us, perhaps, to direct our first sexual impulse towards our mother and our first hatred and our first murderous wish against our father. Our dreams convince us that this is so. . . . But, more fortunate than he, we have meanwhile succeeded, in so far as we have not become psychoneurotics, in detaching our sexual impulses from our mothers and in forgetting our jealousy of our fathers. . . .
>
> While the poet, as he unravels the past, brings to light the guilt of Oedipus, he is at the same time compelling us to recognize our own inner minds, in which those same impulses, though suppressed, are still to be found. . . . Like Oedipus, we live in ignorance of these wishes, repugnant to morality, which have been forced upon us by Nature, and after their revelation we may all of us well seek to close our eyes to the scenes of our childhood.[20]

Once again we come upon the inescapable theme of guilt. Just as in the Sophoclean drama the fearful question is asked —"Where is the dark and barely discernible trace of ancient guilt to be found?"—so every one of us is called upon to find and avow his own guilt.

Guilt and expectation of punishment are thus among the other important factors that drive and guide us toward the solution of this complex during our childhood development. How these processes run their course, what inner transformation is needed for this solution and detachment, has already been indicated. As Freud says:

> The object-cathexes are given up and replaced by identifications. The authority of the father or the parents is introjected into the ego, and there it forms the nucleus of the super-ego, which takes over the severity of the father and

20. *The Interpretation of Dreams* (1900), S.E. IV/V, 262 f.

perpetuates his prohibition against incest, and so secures the ego from the return of the libidinal object-cathexis. The libidinal trends belonging to the Oedipus complex are in part desexualized and sublimated (a thing which probably happens with every transformation into an identification) and in part inhibited in their aim and changed into impulses of affection.[21]

> *The broad general outcome of the sexual phase dominated by the Oedipus complex may, therefore, be taken to be the forming of a precipitate in the ego. . . . This modification of the ego retains its special position; it confronts the other contents of the ego as an ego-ideal or super-ego.*[22]

And now Freud can say:

> Psycho-analysis has been reproached time after time with ignoring the higher, moral, supra-personal side of human nature. The reproach is doubly unjust, both historically and methodologically. For, in the first place, we have from the very beginning attributed the function of instigating repression to the moral and aesthetic trends in the ego, and secondly, there has been a general refusal to recognize that psycho-analytic research could not, like a philosophical system, produce a complete and ready-made theoretical structure, but had to find its way step by step along the path towards understanding the intricacies of the mind by making an analytic dissection of both normal and abnormal phenomena. So long as we had to concern ourselves with the study of what was repressed in mental life, there was no need for us to share in any agitated apprehensions as to the whereabouts of the higher side of man. But now that we have embarked upon the analysis of the ego we can give an answer to all those who have complained that there surely must be a higher nature in man. "Very true," we can say, "and here we have that higher nature, in this ego-ideal or super-ego, the representative of our relation to our parents." When we were little children we knew these higher natures, we admired them and feared them; and later we took them into ourselves.[23]

To the superego, so Freud maintains, we must ascribe self-observation, conscience, and the ideal function. Accordingly,

21. "The Dissolution of the Oedipus Complex" (1924), S.E. XIX, 176 f.
22. "The Ego and the Id," p. 34.
23. *Ibid.*, pp. 35 f.

conscience proves to be a "function" of the superego, and self-observation contains within it "the premise for the judicial activity of conscience," [24] while the ideal function guarantees the building-up of the superego from identifications with various ideals and exemplary models. These three functions are synthesized in the unity of the superego.

Freud's insight into the "trinity" of the superego got differentiated only gradually, as the result of further investigations. For a long time he repeatedly used superego, ego-ideal, and conscience in almost the same sense, although in most cases the shadings between them cannot escape the attentive reader.

"Owing to the way in which the ego-ideal is formed, it has the most abundant links with the phylogenetic acquisition of each individual—his archaic heritage. What has belonged to the lowest part of the mental life of each of us is changed, through the formation of the ideal, into what is highest in the human mind by our scale of values." [25] "The super-ego is the representative for us of every moral restriction, the advocate of a striving towards perfection—it is, in short, as much as we have been able to grasp psychologically of what is described as the higher side of human life." It is the precipitate of everything that parents, teachers, and exemplary models have inculcated into us; later it also incarnates the ideals, the moral decencies, the spiritual currents we have absorbed into ourselves. Thus "it becomes the vehicle of tradition and of all the time-resisting judgments of value which have propagated themselves in this manner from generation to generation. . . . The past, the tradition of the race and of the people, lives on in the ideologies of the super-ego." [26]

"Through the forming of the ideal, what biology and the vicissitudes of the human species have created in the id and left behind in it is taken over by the ego and individually re-

24. A. M. Becker, "Zur Gliederung des Ueber-Ichs," in *Entfaltung der Psychoanalyse* (Stuttgart, 1957), p. 94.
25. "The Ego and the Id," p. 36.
26. *New Introductory Lectures on Psycho-Analysis,* pp. 66 f.

experienced." [27] This will become of crucial significance also in the history of a people, indeed of mankind as a whole. In tradition, moral and ethical demands as well as new goals of reform constantly break through in the shape of a leader-figure or "idea" that imposes itself on the masses as an ego-ideal and embodies that ideal for them. [28]

Thus the superego appears to be the trustee of all that human history has laid down in us as a heritage and as a new creation. It is not only the administrator of this property; it is also a creative reformer and innovator.

WE HAVE NOW COME TO KNOW the superego, not exhaustively, to be sure, but only with respect to what actually concerns us here, namely, conscience. The superego is the agency, the locus, from which conscience works. If hitherto we have stressed only its severity, which pronounces the verdict "guilty," we ourselves have been guilty of one-sidedness. The recognition alone that it is the administrator and creative reformer of traditional values is enough to reveal to us its synthetic activity under the guidance of Eros, love. If the imago of the parents and of parental authority is introjected into the superego, so also is their love and our love for them, together with the ideals that they and their imagos have transmitted to us. When we said at the beginning that the superego not only *judges* man but also *directs* him, we did so because our ideals operate in it as dictates and exemplary models, ideals not acquired only in the course of our individual lives, not handed down only by tradition, but representing for a large part our archaic heritage. Supported by this insight, Freud speaks also of an ego-ideal or ideal ego which likewise belongs to the superego. We should not forget that it is always our *ego* that orients itself by these ideal dictates and inner laws—that takes them over and carries them out—provided it has the necessary

27. "The Ego and the Id," p. 36.
28. Cf. Freud, *Group Psychology and the Analysis of the Ego* (1921), S.E. XVIII.

strength or can bring itself to maturity by constantly measuring itself against its ideal.

These ideals are not rigid norms. Rather, they are ideal images, ideal symbols, and as such are capable of representing eternal values. Jung has coined the term "archetype" for these psychic contents. Erich Neumann describes conscience in this sense as the "collectively determined superego component of the father archetype." [29]

Although the ego-ideals toward which the ego strives can be regarded as a phylogenetic and ontogenetic heritage and can even be proved to be such, they should nevertheless, in their interaction with the ego, do justice to man's actual striving in relation to outer and inner reality. In this inner dialogue between ego and ideal is fulfilled his authentic existence as a human being. Man does not experience himself only as a creature flung into passion and pathos; he discovers himself also in being called upon to attain maturity and greater stature, and he struggles just as passionately—a demand he makes upon himself—toward his goals. The choice of goal and the struggle make the man and qualify him. This choice ensues from the criteria and ideals which are set for him or which he sets for himself. It requires continual self-measurement and continual challenge. In this self-measurement and challenge we experience our conscience.

We can now come back with more understanding to a point we mentioned at the beginning: that Freud describes conscience as exercising a directing function toward what is "right," that is, toward the ego-ideal. "With this end in view, [it] constantly watches the actual ego and measures it by that ideal . . . ; what we call our 'conscience' has the required characteristics. . . . For what prompted the subject to form an ego-ideal, on whose behalf his conscience acts as a watchman . . . ?" [30] For Freud this conscience is also an irrational agency. It speaks continually to us but does not address itself

29. Erich Neumann, *The Origins and History of Consciousness* (New York and London, 1954), p. 183.
30. "On Narcissism: An Introduction," pp. 95 f.

to the real guilt. On the contrary, the truly guiltless person is harder hit by conscience than is the unscrupulous one who for that very reason has "no conscience." "For the more virtuous a man is, the more severe and distrustful is its behaviour, so that ultimately it is precisely those people who have carried saintliness furthest who reproach themselves for the worst sinfulness." [31] The tension between ego and conscience expresses itself as guilt feeling, which is now no longer a reaction to a bad deed but a challenge to accept life as a person who admits his guilt. The agreement of Freud's views with those of Heidegger, Jaspers, Kierkegaard, and other existential philosophers and psychologists is striking.

We come now to the "other side" of our observations, having said at the beginning that psychoanalysis is situated between biology and existential anthropology and passes over into both.

The analytical psychotherapist finds guilt and conscience joined in indissoluble union. The voice of conscience can be heard only in the ambience of guiltiness; otherwise it speaks "in the mode of silence" (Heidegger).[32] It is the sense of guilt that makes conscience perceptible, so that we experience it as a plague and a torment. Admittedly, this is only one side of it, for, as we have seen, conscience is concerned with inner and outer reconciliation under the guidance of love. But there can be no doubt that conscience about the sense of guilt and its need for punishment can be cruel and agonizing. Only with the interiorization and introjection of aggressiveness, its alliance with Eros, and its sublimation does conscience become a *moral* agency. We now eschew injustice and evil, not because they are forbidden, not because of the threat of punishment and the withdrawal of love, but because of an inner command coming from within. The primitive sense of guilt that springs from the fear of authority changes into our own inner guilti-

31. *Civilization and Its Discontents*, pp. 125 f.
32. Martin Heidegger, *Sein und Zeit* (Halle: Max Niemeyer, 1941); English translation, *Being and Time*, trans. John Macquarrie and Edward Robinson (New York: Harper, 1962).

ness, which forces us to conduct an inner dialogue between ego and superego. We can now assess how important this insight is into the function of conscience in all manifestations of moral discord and breakdown, whether they be pathological or an expression of human failure and error in the struggle with our passions. Our whole endeavor, therapeutic or educational or broadly "social," is to guide man toward an interiorization of social and ethical demands, which consists not only in the building of a harmonious superego agency, not only in the formation of an ego, but in the maturation of an ego-figure in which ego and superego complement each other and bring each other to fulfillment. This is, in the last resort, what our conscience is endeavoring to do. Out of this endeavor grows its very essence, which, in Freud's own words, is "the readiness to feel guilty." [33] With that definition Freud has united his basic conception of conscience with the teachings of philosophy and theology. For this "readiness to feel guilty" is just as much a requirement of our religion and our piety as Heidegger's admonition to "want to have conscience." [34]

HERE I COULD BRING my remarks to an end. But I would be denying my better ego, so to speak, if I were to give voice only to the psychologist in me and not to the doctor, the psychotherapist, as well. The application of our insights to psychotherapy would, however, be a chapter in itself.

We have defined the psychic sufferer as a person caught in a conflict of conscience. Let us elaborate on this theme:

> Deluded in the vital sphere of his being, he gives his actions a false meaning, so is unable to turn them into *genuine* actions and has to make do with mere activities. . . . Nor does he achieve a realization of himself, but only a compensatory satisfaction. He is the victim of his fate, of the being he has become, whom he can neither conquer nor accept. . . . Nor can he accept his guilt, but only a partial guilt. He himself isn't guilty, but only feels guilty, has guilt feelings. This

33. *Civilization and Its Discontents*, p. 131.
34. *Sein und Zeit*, p. 288; *Being and Time*, p. 334.

guilty feeling is transposed into feeling sick, and so, caught in a circle from which there is no escape, he submits himself to continual self-punishment. He flees from the truth of guilt into the untruth of his sickness. But even sickness could be true: as suffering. He accepts this sickness as little as his guilt; he cannot accept it, because it is not a genuine sickness, not authentic, true suffering. . . .

But in sickness a man has to accept his guilt, and the doctor has to show him the way. Not only because he has to accept everything that enters his life, and everything he accepts is guilt, but because he is actually an accomplice in all sickness. Sickness is never imposed from outside, as though by an alien force, by Nature. The religious person has always taken sickness as guilt and a test; and though it is laid upon him by a higher power, he is yet guilty of it because he is human. Guilt is man's privilege.[35]

Or, in Scheler's words: "If anyone were to say 'I am not conscious of any guilt so have nothing to regret,' he would be either a god or an animal. But if the speaker is a human being, then he knows nothing of the nature of guilt." [36] Buber says:

Anyone who rids himself of this guilt gets into the deficiency of sickness because of *not wanting* to be guilty. He does not heed the voice of conscience calling him to *be* guilty. But the continually unfulfilled and unfulfillable call to *be* guilty is unendurable. Consequently guiltiness turns into *feeling* guilty and the call of conscience into punishment, while guilt itself becomes a demonstrative symptom of being hindered, a demonstration of the "inability" to follow the call of conscience. And yet what alone matters is that life should be lived from the fact of guilt, not indeed as a life of expiation, but rather of at-one-ment, a life that makes amends, that makes good.[37]

We may say, further: "In the therapeutic situation this 'making good' is the cure. . . . By fulfilling the dictates of conscience we exchange guiltiness for an avowal of responsi-

35. Ernst Blum, "Grundsätzliches zur psychotherapeutischen Situation," *Psyche*, VI (1952–53), 552. Cf. O. Schwartz, *Medizinische Anthropologie* (Leipzig: S. Hirzel, 1929), p. 328.
36. Quoted from H. Haefner, *Schulderleben und Gewissen* (Stuttgart, 1956).
37. Martin Buber, "Geleitwort zu Hans Trüb," *Heilung aus der Begegnung* (Stuttgart: Ernst Klett, 1951), p. 10.

bility to ourselves and others. This in turn is a step towards healing." [38]

What is the role and task of the doctor here? He must make the patient clairaudient to the call of conscience and capable of guilt. In psychoanalytic terms, that means arousing and consolidating the essential relations between ego and ideal, creating a synthesis between ego, superego, and the passions. In other words, the "doctor as conscience" and "conscience as doctor" should guide the patient toward "that of which he is most certainly conscious." The patient must continually prove to the doctor his own potentialities for conscience and, helped by the conscientious demands of the doctor, must pull himself back from deterioration, dereliction, and inauthenticity. The doctor thus stands, in the end, for the function of conscience. Freud's own view bears this out: that it is the doctor who, like conscience, unremittingly watches "the actual ego" and measures it by the ideal.

In his last and uncompleted work Freud recapitulates this conception: "The ego is weakened by the internal conflict, and we must go to its help. . . . The analytic physician and the patient's weakened ego, basing themselves on the real external world, have to band themselves together into a party against the enemies, the instinctual demands of the id and the conscientious demands of the super-ego." [39] This means that, as psychotherapists, we have not only to strengthen the ego of the patient but to mitigate the severity of the superego. This is the "function" of the doctor; this is the "function" of conscience which the doctor takes upon himself.

38. Blum, *op. cit.*, pp. 552 f.
39. *An Outline of Psycho-Analysis* (1938), S.E. XXIII, 173.

A Psychological View
of Conscience

C. G. Jung

Translated by R. F. C. Hull

THE ETYMOLOGY of the word "conscience" tells us that it is a special form of "knowledge" or "consciousness." [1] The peculiarity of "conscience" is that it is a knowledge of, or certainty about, the emotional value of the ideas we have concerning the motives of our actions. According to this definition, conscience is a complex phenomenon consisting on the one hand in an elementary act of the will, or in an impulse to act for which no conscious reason can be given, and on the other hand in a judgment grounded on rational feeling. This judgment is a value judgment, and it differs from an intellectual judgment in that, besides having an objective, general, and impartial character, it reveals the subjective point of reference. A value judgment always implicates the subject, presupposing that something is good or beautiful *for me*. If, on the other hand, I say that it is good or beautiful for certain other people, this is not necessarily a value judgment but may just as well be an intellectual statement of fact. Conscience, therefore, is made up of two layers, the lower one comprising a particular psychic

This translation was first published in *Civilization in Transition*, Volume X of *The Collected Works of C. G. Jung*, Bollingen Series XX (New York: Pantheon Books, 1964), pp. 437–55, and is reprinted here by permission of the Bollingen Foundation, Routledge & Kegan Paul Ltd., and by the heirs of Dr. Jung.
1. [In the original, respectively, *Gewissen, Wissen,* and *Bewusstsein.* Cf. Lat. *conscientia, scientia* (from *scire,* "to know"), *conscius.*—TRANSLATOR.]

event, while the upper one is a kind of superstructure representing the positive or negative judgment of the subject.

As we might expect from the complexity of the phenomenon, its empirical phenomenology covers a very wide field. Conscience may appear as an act of conscious reflection which anticipates, accompanies, or follows certain psychic events, or as a mere emotional concomitant of them, in which case its moral character is not immediately evident. Thus, an apparently groundless anxiety state may follow a certain action, without the subject being conscious of the least connection between them. Often the moral judgment is displaced into a dream which the subject does not understand. For example, a businessman I knew was made what looked like a perfectly serious and honorable offer which, it turned out much later, would have involved him in a disastrous fraud had he accepted it. The following night after he received this offer, which as I say seemed to him quite acceptable, he dreamt that his hands and forearms were covered with black dirt. He could see no connection with the events of the previous day, because he was unable to admit to himself that the offer had touched him on the vulnerable spot: his expectation of a good business deal. I warned him about this, and he was careful enough to take certain precautions which did in fact save him from more serious harm. Had he examined the situation right at the beginning he would undoubtedly have had a bad conscience, for he would have understood that it was a "dirty business" which his morality would not have allowed him to touch. He would, as we say, have made his hands dirty. The dream represented this locution in pictorial form.

In this instance the classical characteristic of conscience, the *conscientia peccati* ("consciousness of sin"), is missing. Accordingly the specific feeling-tone of a bad conscience is missing too. Instead, the symbolical image of black hands appeared in a dream, calling his attention to some dirty work. In order to become conscious of his moral reaction, i.e., to feel his conscience, he had to tell the dream to me. This was an act of conscience on his part, insofar as dreams always made him feel rather uncertain. He had got this feeling of uncertainty in the course of an analysis, which showed him that dreams often contribute a great deal to self-knowledge. Without this experience he would probably have overlooked the dream.

From this we learn one important fact: the moral evaluation of an action, which expresses itself in the specific feeling-tone of the accompanying ideas, is not always dependent on consciousness but may function without it. Freud put forward the hypothesis that in these cases there is a repression exerted by a psychic factor, the so-called superego. But if the conscious mind is to accomplish the voluntary act of repression, we must presuppose that there is some recognition of the moral obnoxiousness of the content to be repressed, for without this motive the corresponding impulse of the will cannot be released. But it was just this knowledge which the businessman lacked, to such an extent that he not only felt no moral reaction but put only a limited trust in my warning. The reason for this was that he in no way recognized the dubious nature of the offer and therefore lacked any motive for repression. Hence the hypothesis of conscious repression cannot apply in this case.

What happened was in reality an unconscious act which accomplished itself as though it were conscious and intentional —as though, in other words, it were an act of conscience. It is as if the subject recognized the immorality of the offer and this recognition had released the appropriate emotional reaction. But the entire process took place subliminally, and the only trace it left behind was the dream, which, as a moral reaction, remained unconscious. "Conscience," in the sense in which we defined it above, as a "knowledge" of the ego, a *conscientia*, simply does not exist in this case. If conscience is a kind of knowledge, then it is not the empirical subject who is the knower, but rather an unconscious personality who, to all appearances, behaves like a conscious subject. It knows the dubious nature of the offer, it recognizes the acquisitive greed of the ego, which does not shrink even from illegality, and it causes the appropriate judgment to be pronounced. This means that the ego has been replaced by an unconscious personality who performs the necessary act of conscience.

It was these and similar experiences which led Freud to endow the superego with special significance. The Freudian superego is not, however, a natural and inherited part of the psyche's structure; it is rather the consciously acquired stock of traditional customs, the "moral code" as incorporated, for instance, in the Ten Commandments. The superego is a patriarchal legacy which, as such, is a conscious acquisition and an equally conscious possession. If it appears to be an almost unconscious factor in Freud's writings, this is due to his practical experience, which taught him that, in a surprising number of cases, the act of conscience takes place unconsciously, as in our example. Freud and his school rejected the hypothesis of inherited, instinctive modes of behavior, termed by us archetypes, as mystical and unscientific, and accordingly explained unconscious acts of conscience as repressions caused by the superego.

The concept of the superego contains nothing that, in itself, would not be recognized as belonging to the common stock of thought. To that extent it is identical with what we call the "moral code." The only peculiar thing about it is that one or the other aspect of the moral tradition proves unconscious in the individual case. We should also mention that Freud admitted the existence of "archaic vestiges" in the superego—of acts of conscience, therefore, which are influenced by archaic motifs. But since Freud disputed the existence of archetypes, that is, of genuine archaic modes of behavior, we can only assume that by "archaic vestiges" he meant certain conscious traditions which may be unconscious in certain individuals. In no circumstances can it be a question of inborn types, for otherwise they would be, on his own hypothesis, inherited ideas. But that is just what he does mean, though so far as I know there are no proofs of their existence. There are, however, proofs in abundance for the hypothesis of inherited, instinctive modes of behavior, namely, the archetypes. It is therefore probable that the "archaic vestiges" in the superego are a concession to the archetypes theory and imply a fundamental doubt as to the absolute dependence of unconscious contents on consciousness. There are indeed good grounds for doubting this dependence: first, the unconscious is, ontogenetically and phylogenetically, older than consciousness, and secondly, it is a well-known fact that it can hardly be influenced, if at all, by the conscious will. It can only be repressed or suppressed, and only temporarily at that. As a rule its account has to be settled sooner or later. Were that not so, psychotherapy would be no problem. If the unconscious were dependent on consciousness, we could, by insight and application of the will, finally get the better of the unconscious, and the psyche could be completely remodeled to suit our purpose. Only unworldly idealists, rationalists, and other fanatics can indulge in such dreams. The psyche is a phenomenon not subject to our will; it is nature, and though nature can, by skill, knowledge, and patience, be modified at a few points, it cannot be changed into something artificial without profound injury to our humanity. Man can be transformed into a sick animal but not molded into an intellectual ideal.

Although people still labor under the delusion that consciousness represents the whole of the psychic man, it is nevertheless only a part, of whose relation to the whole we know very little. Since the unconscious component really is unconscious, no boundaries can be assigned to it: we cannot say where the psyche begins or ends. We know that consciousness and its contents are the modifiable part of the psyche, but the more deeply we seek to penetrate, at least indirectly, into the realm of the unconscious, the more the impression forces itself on us that we are dealing with something autonomous. We must admit that our best results, whether in education or treatment, occur when the unconscious cooperates, that is to say, when the goal we are aiming at coincides with the unconscious trend of development, and that, conversely, our best methods and intentions fail when nature does not come to our aid. Without at least some degree of autonomy the common experience of the complementary or compensatory function of the unconscious would not be possible. If the unconscious were really dependent on the conscious, it could not contain more than, and other things than, consciousness contains.

Our dream-example and many other cases of the kind suggest that, since the subliminal moral judgment accords with the moral code, the dream has behaved in the same way as a consciousness backed by traditional moral law, and that, consequently, ordinary morality is a basic law of the unconscious or at any rate influences it. This conclusion stands in flagrant contradiction to the common experience of the autonomy of the unconscious. Although morality as such is a universal attribute of the human psyche, the same cannot be maintained of a given moral code. It cannot, therefore, be an integral part of the psyche's structure. Nevertheless, the fact remains—as our example shows—that the act of conscience operates, in principle, in exactly the same way in the unconscious as in the conscious, follows the same moral precepts, and therefore evokes the impression that the moral code also controls the unconscious process.

This impression is deceptive, because in practice there are just as many, and perhaps even more, examples where the subliminal reaction does not conform at all to the moral code. Thus I was once consulted by a very distinguished lady—distinguished not only for her irreproachable conduct but also for her intensely "spiritual" attitude—on account of her "revolting" dreams. Her dreams did indeed deserve this epithet. She produced a whole series of extremely unsavory dream-images all about drunken prostitutes, venereal diseases, and a lot more besides. She was horrified by these obscenities and could not understand why she, who had always striven for the highest, should be haunted by these apparitions from the abyss. She might just as well have asked why the saints are exposed to the vilest temptations. Here the moral code plays the contrary role —if it plays any role at all. Far from uttering moral exhortations, the unconscious delights in spawning every conceivable immorality, as though it had what was morally repulsive exclusively in mind. Experiences of this sort are so common and so regular that even Saint Paul could confess: "For the good that I would I do not, but the evil which I would not, that I do" (Rom. 7:19).

In view of the fact that dreams lead astray as much as they exhort, it seems doubtful whether what appears to be a judgment of conscience should be evaluated as such—in other words, whether we should attribute to the unconscious a function which appears moral to us. Obviously we can understand dreams in a moral sense without at the same time assuming that the unconscious, too, connects them with any moral tendency. It seems, rather, that it pronounces moral judgments with the same objectivity with which it produces immoral fantasies. This paradox, or inner contradictoriness of conscience, has long been known to investigators of this question: besides the "right" kind of conscience there is a "wrong" one, which exaggerates, perverts, and twists evil into good and good into evil just as our own scruples do; and it does so with the same compulsiveness and with the same emotional consequences as the "right" kind of conscience. Were it not for this paradox, the question of conscience would present no problem; we could then rely wholly on its decisions so far as morality is concerned. But since there is great and justified uncertainty in this regard, it needs unusual courage or—what amounts to the same thing—unshakable faith for a person simply to follow the dictates of his own conscience. As a rule one obeys only up to a certain point, which is determined in advance by the moral code. This is where those dreaded conflicts of duty begin. Generally they are answered according to the precepts of the moral code, but only in a very few cases are they really decided by an individual act of judgment. For as soon as the moral code ceases to act as a support, conscience easily succumbs to a fit of weakness.

In practice it is indeed very difficult to distinguish conscience from the traditional moral precepts. For this reason it is often thought that conscience is nothing more than the suggestive effect of these precepts, and that it would not exist if no moral laws had been invented. But the phenomenon we call "conscience" is found at every level of human culture. Whether an Eskimo has a bad conscience about skinning an animal with an iron knife instead of the traditional flint one, or about leaving a friend in the lurch whom he ought to help, in both cases he feels an inner reproach, a "twinge of conscience," and in both cases the deviation from an inveterate habit or generally accepted rule produces something like a shock. For the primitive psyche anything unusual or not customary causes an emotional reaction, and the more it runs counter to the "collective representations" which almost invariably govern the prescribed mode of behavior, the more violent the reaction will be. It is a peculiarity of the primitive mind to endow everything with mythical derivations that are meant to explain it. Thus everything that we would call pure chance is understood to be intentional and is regarded as a magical influence. Such explanations are in no sense "inventions"; they are spontaneous fantasy-products which appear without premeditation in a natural and quite involuntary way; unconscious, archetypal reactions such as are peculiar to the human psyche. Nothing could be more mistaken than to assume that a myth is something "thought up." It comes into existence of its own accord, as can be observed in all authentic products of fantasy, and particularly in dreams. It is the hybris of consciousness to pretend that everything derives from *its* primacy, despite the fact that consciousness itself demonstrably comes from an older unconscious psyche. The unity and continuity of consciousness are such late acquisitions that there is still a fear that they might get lost again.

So, too, our moral reactions exemplify the original behavior of the psyche, while moral laws are a late concomitant of moral behavior, congealed into precepts. In consequence, they appear to be identical with the moral reaction, that is, with conscience. This delusion becomes obvious the moment a conflict of duty makes clear the difference between conscience and the moral code. It will then be decided which is the stronger: tradition and conventional morality, or conscience.

Am I to tell the truth and thereby involve a fellow human being in catastrophe, or should I tell a lie in order to save a human life? In such dilemmas we are certainly not obeying our conscience if we stick obstinately and in all circumstances to the commandment: Thou shalt not lie. We have merely observed the moral code. But if we obey the judgment of conscience, we stand alone and have hearkened to a subjective voice, not knowing what the motives are on which it rests. No one can guarantee that he has only noble motives. We know —some of us—far too much about ourselves to pretend that we are one hundred per cent good and not egotists to the marrow. Always behind what we imagine are our best deeds stands the devil, patting us paternally on the shoulder and whispering, "Well done!"

Where does the true and authentic conscience, which rises above the moral code and refuses to submit to its dictates, get its justification from? What gives it the courage to assume that it is not a false conscience, a self-deception?

John says: "Try the spirits whether they are of God" (I John 4:1), an admonition we could profitably apply to ourselves. Since olden times conscience has been understood by many people less as a psychic function than as a divine intervention; indeed, its dictates were regarded as *vox Dei*, the voice of God. This view shows what value and significance were, and still are, attached to the phenomenon of conscience. The psychologist cannot disregard such an evaluation, for it too is a well-authenticated phenomenon that must be taken into account if we want to treat the idea of conscience psychologically. The question of "truth," which is usually raised here in a quite nonobjective way, as to whether it has been proved that God himself speaks to us with the voice of conscience, has nothing to do with the psychological problem. The *vox Dei* is an assertion and an opinion, like the assertion that there is such a thing as conscience at all. All psychological facts which cannot be verified with the help of scientific apparatus and exact methods of measurement are assertions and opinions, and, as such, are psychic realities. It is a *psychological truth* that the opinion exists that the voice of conscience is the voice of God.

Since, then, the phenomenon of conscience in itself does not coincide with the moral code, but is anterior to it, transcends its contents, and, as already mentioned, can also be "false," the view of conscience as the voice of God becomes an extremely delicate problem. In practice it is very difficult to indicate the exact point at which the "right" conscience stops and the "false" one begins and what the criterion is that divides one from the other. Presumably it is the moral code again, which makes it its business to know exactly what is good and what is evil. But if the voice of conscience is the voice of God, this voice must possess an incomparably higher authority than traditional morality. Anyone, therefore, who allows conscience this status should, for better or worse, put his trust in divine guidance and follow his conscience rather than give heed to conventional morality. If the believer had absolute confidence in his definition of God as the Summum Bonum, it would be easy for him to obey the inner voice, for he could be sure of never being led astray. But since, in the Lord's Prayer, we still beseech God not to lead us into temptation, this undermines the very trust the believer should have if, in the darkness of a conflict of duty, he is to obey the voice of conscience without regard to the "world" and, very possibly, act against the precepts of the moral code by "obeying God rather than men" (Acts 5:29).

Conscience—no matter on what it is based—commands the individual to obey his inner voice even at the risk of going astray. We can refuse to obey this command by an appeal to the moral code and the moral views on which it is founded, though with an uncomfortable feeling of having been disloyal. One may think what one likes about an ethos, yet an ethos is and remains an inner value, injury to which is no joke and can sometimes have very serious psychic consequences. These, admittedly, are known to relatively few people, for there are only a few who take objective account of psychic causality. The psyche is one of those things which people know least about, because no one likes to inquire into his own shadow. Even psychology is misused for the purpose of concealing the true causal connections from oneself. The more "scientific" it pretends to be, the more welcome is its so-called objectivity, because this is an excellent way of getting rid of the inconvenient emotional components of conscience, notwithstanding that these are the real dynamics of the moral reaction. Without its emotional dynamism the phenomenon of conscience loses all meaning—which is, of course, the unconscious goal of the so-called "scientific" approach.

Conscience is, in itself, an autonomous psychic factor. All statements which do not directly deny it are agreed on this point. The clearest in this regard is the *vox Dei* concept. Here conscience is the voice of God, which often cuts sharply across our subjective intentions and may sometimes force an extremely disagreeable decision. If Freud himself attributed an almost daemonic power to the superego, although by definition it is not even a genuine conscience but merely human convention and tradition, this is in no sense an exaggeration: he was simply confirming the regular experience of the practicing psychologist. Conscience is a demand that asserts itself in spite of the subject, or at any rate causes him considerable difficulties. This is not to deny that there are cases of lack of conscience. But the idea that conscience as such is only something learnt can be maintained only by those who imagine they were present on those prehistoric occasions when the first moral reactions came into existence. Conscience is far from being the only instance of an inner factor autonomously opposing the will of the subject. Every complex does that, and no one in his right senses would declare that it was "learnt" and that nobody would have a complex if it had not been hammered into him. Even domestic animals, to whom we erroneously deny a conscience, have complexes and moral reactions.

Primitive man regards the autonomy of the psyche as demonism and magic. This, we consider, is only what one would expect in primitive society. On closer inspection one finds, however, that the civilized man of antiquity, such as Socrates, still had his daemon and that there was a widespread and natural belief in superhuman beings who, we would suppose today, were personifications of projected unconscious contents. This belief has not, in principle, disappeared, but still persists in numerous variants. For instance, in the assumption that conscience is the voice of God, or that it is a very important psychic factor (and one which manifests itself according to temperament, seeing that it usually accompanies the most differentiated function, as in the case of a "thinking" or a "feeling" morality). Again, where conscience seems to play no role, it appears indirectly in the form of compulsions or obsessions. These manifestations all go to show that the moral reaction is the outcome of an autonomous dynamism, fittingly called man's daemon, genius, guardian angel, better self, heart, inner voice, the inner and higher man, and so forth. Close beside these, beside the positive, "right" conscience, there stands the negative, "false" conscience called the devil, seducer, tempter, evil spirit, etc. Everyone who examines his conscience is confronted with this fact, and he must admit that the good exceeds the bad only by a very little, if at all. It is therefore quite in order for Saint Paul to admit to having his "messenger of Satan" (II Corinthians 12:7). We ought to avoid sin and occasionally we can; but, as experience shows, we fall into sin again at the very next step. Only unconscious and wholly uncritical people can imagine it possible to abide in a permanent state of moral goodness. But because most people are devoid of self-criticism, permanent self-deception is the rule. A more developed consciousness brings the latent moral conflict to light, or else sharpens those opposites which are already conscious. Reason enough to eschew self-knowledge and psychology altogether and to treat the psyche with contempt!

There is scarcely any other psychic phenomenon that shows the polarity of the psyche in a clearer light than conscience. Its undoubted dynamism, in order to be understood at all, can only be explained in terms of energy, that is, as a potential based on opposites. Conscience brings these ever-present and necessary opposites to conscious perception. It would be a great mistake to suppose that one could ever get rid of this polarity, for it is an essential element in the psychic structure. Even if the moral reaction could be eliminated by training, the opposites would simply use a mode of expression other than the moral one. They would still continue to exist. But if the *vox Dei* conception of conscience is correct, we are faced logically with a metaphysical dilemma: either there is a dualism, and God's omnipotence is halved, or the opposites are contained in the monotheistic God-image, as for instance in the Old Testament image of Yahweh, which shows us morally contradictory opposites existing side by side. This figure corresponds to a unitary image of the psyche dynamically based on opposites, like Plato's charioteer driving the white and the black horses. Alternatively, we must admit with Faust: "Two souls, alas, are housed within my breast," which no human charioteer can master, as the fate of Faust clearly indicates.

The psychologist can criticize metaphysics as a human assertion, but he is not in a position to make such assertions himself. He can only establish that these assertions exist as a kind of exclamation, well knowing that neither one nor the other can be proved right and objectively valid, although he must acknowledge the legitimacy of subjective assertions as such. Assertions of this kind are manifestations of the psyche which belong to our human nature, and there is no psychic wholeness without them, even though one can grant them no more than subjective validity. Thus the *vox Dei* hypothesis is another subjective exclamation, whose purpose it is to underline the numinous character of the moral reaction. Conscience is a manifestation of *mana*, of the "extraordinarily powerful," a quality which is the especial peculiarity of archetypal ideas. For, insofar as the moral reaction is only apparently identical with the suggestive effect of the moral code, it falls within the sphere of the collective unconscious, exemplifying an archetypal pattern of behavior reaching down into the animal psyche. Experience shows that the archetype, as a natural phenomenon, has a morally ambivalent character, or rather, it possesses no moral quality in itself but is amoral, like the Yahwistic God-image, and acquires moral qualities only through the act of cognition. Thus Yahweh is both just and unjust, kindly and cruel, truthful and deceitful. This is eminently true of the archetype as well. That is why the primitive form of conscience is paradoxical: to burn a heretic is on the one hand a pious and meritorious act—as John Hus himself ironically recognized when, bound to the stake, he espied an old woman hobbling toward him with a bundle of faggots, and exclaimed, "O sancta simplicitas!"—and on the other hand a brutal manifestation of ruthless and savage lust for revenge.

Both forms of conscience, the right and the false, stem from the same source, and both therefore have approximately the same power of conviction. This is also apparent in the symbolic designation of Christ as Lucifer ("bringer of light"), lion, raven (or *nycticorax:* night-heron), serpent, son of God, etc., all of which he shares with Satan; in the idea that the good father-god of Christianity is so vindictive that it takes the cruel sacrifice of his son to reconcile him to humanity; in the belief that the Summum Bonum has a tendency to lead such an inferior and helpless creature as man into temptation, only to consign him to eternal damnation if he is not astute enough to spot the divine trap. Faced with these insufferable paradoxes, which are an affront to our religious feelings, I would suggest reducing the notion of the *vox Dei* to the hypothesis of the archetype, for this at least is understandable and accessible to investigation. The archetype is a pattern of behavior that has always existed, that is morally indifferent as a biological phenomenon, but possesses a powerful dynamism by means of which it can profoundly influence human behavior.

The concept of the archetype has been misunderstood so often that one can hardly mention it without having to explain in anew each time. It is derived from the repeated observation that, for instance, the myths and fairy tales of world literature contain definite motifs which crop up everywhere. We meet these same motifs in the fantasies, dreams, deliriums, and delusions of individuals living today. These typical images and associations are what I call archetypal ideas. The more vivid they are, the more they will be colored by particularly strong feeling-tones. This accentuation gives them a special dynamism in our psychic life. They impress, influence, and fascinate us. They have their origin in the archetype, which in itself is an irrepresentable, unconscious, pre-existent form that seems to be part of the inherited structure of the psyche and can therefore manifest itself spontaneously anywhere, at any time. Because of its instinctual nature, the archetype underlies the feeling-toned complexes and shares their autonomy. It is also the psychic precondition of religious assertions and is responsible for the anthropomorphism of all God-images. This fact, however, affords no ground for any metaphysical judgment, whether positive or negative.

With this view we remain within the framework of what can be experienced and known. The *vox Dei* hypothesis is then no more than an amplificatory tendency peculiar to the archetype—a mythological statement inseparably bound up with numinous experiences which expresses these occurrences and also seeks to explain them. By reducing them to something empirically knowable, we do not in any way prejudice their transcendence. When, for example, someone was struck by lightning, the man of antiquity believed that Zeus had hurled a thunderbolt at him. Instead of this mythical dramatization we content ourselves with the more modest explanation that a sudden discharge of electrical tension happened to take place just at the spot where this unlucky man stood under a tree. The weak point in this argument, of course, is the so-called "accident," about which several things could be said. On the primitive level there are no accidents of this sort, but only intentional designs.

The reduction of the act of conscience to a collision with the archetype is, by and large, a tenable explanation. On the other hand we must admit that the *psychoid* archetype,[2] that is,

2. [Concerning the "psychoid" factor see "On the Nature of the Psyche," in *The Structure and Dynamics of the Psyche, Collected Works,* VIII (1960), 176 f., 183 f., 213.—TRANSLATOR.]

its irrepresentable and unconscious essence, is not just a postulate only, but possesses qualities of a parapsychological nature which I have grouped together under the term "synchronicity." I use this term to indicate the fact that, in cases of telepathy, precognition, and similar inexplicable phenomena, one can very frequently observe an archetypal situation. This may be connected with the collective nature of the archetype, for the collective unconscious, unlike the personal unconscious, is one and the same everywhere, in all individuals, just as all biological functions and all instincts are the same in members of the same species. Apart from the more subtle *synchronicity*,[3] we can also observe in the instincts, for instance in the migratory instinct, a distinct *synchronism*. And since the parapsychological phenomena associated with the unconscious psyche show a peculiar tendency to relativize the categories of time and space, the collective unconscious must have a spaceless and timeless quality. Consequently, there is some probability that an archetypal situation will be accompanied by synchronistic phenomena, as in the case of death, in whose vicinity such phenomena are relatively frequent.

As with all archetypal phenomena, the synchronicity factor must be taken into account in considering conscience. For although the voice of genuine conscience (and not just the recollection of the moral code) may make itself heard in the context of an archetypal situation, it is by no means certain that the reason for this is always a subjective moral reaction. It sometimes happens that a person suffers from a decidedly bad conscience for no demonstrable reason. Naturally there are any number of cases where ignorance and self-deception offer a sufficient explanation. But this does not alter the fact that one can suddenly have a bad conscience when one is conversing with an unknown person who would have every reason to feel a bad conscience but is unconscious of it. The same is true of fear and other emotions arising from a collision with an arche-

3. [Cf. "Synchronicity: An Acausal Connecting Principle," *ibid.*— TRANSLATOR.]

type. When one is talking with somebody whose unconscious contents are "constellated," a parallel constellation arises in one's own unconscious. The same or a similar archetype is activated, and since one is less unconscious than the other person and has no reason for repression, one becomes increasingly aware of its feeling-tone in the form of a growing uneasiness of conscience. When this happens, we naturally tend to ascribe the moral reaction to ourselves, the more easily since no one, actually, has reason to enjoy a perfectly good conscience. But in the case we are discussing, the self-criticism, laudable in itself, goes too far. We discover that, as soon as the conversation is ended, the bad conscience stops as suddenly as it began, and after a while it turns out that it is the other person who should take note of his bad conscience. By way of example, one thinks of cases like the one described by Heinrich Zschokke.[4] While in Brugg, he visited an inn, where he ate lunch. Opposite him sat a young man. Suddenly Zschokke saw in his mind's eye this young man standing at a desk, breaking it open, and pocketing the money he found. Zschokke even knew the exact amount and was so sure of it that he took the young man to task. The latter was so flabbergasted by Zschokke's knowledge that he made a confession on the spot.

This spontaneous reconstruction of an unknown fact can also be expressed in a dream, or give rise to a disagreeable feeling that cannot be put into words, or cause one to guess a situation without knowing to whom it refers. The psychoid archetype has a tendency to behave as though it were not localized in one person but were active in the whole environment. The fact or situation is transmitted in most cases through a subliminal perception of the affect it produces. Animals and primitives have a particularly fine nose for these things. This explanation, however, does not cover parapsychological events.

Experiences of this kind are the common lot of the psychotherapist, or of anybody who has frequent occasion to talk

4. Johann Heinrich Zschokke, *Eine Selbstschau*, 3d ed. (Aarau, 1843).

professionally, about their intimate affairs, with people with whom he has no personal relationship. One should not conclude from this that every subjective pang of conscience which seems unfounded is caused by the person one is conversing with. Such a conclusion is justified only when the ever-present guilt component in oneself proves, after mature reflection, to be an inadequate explanation of the reaction. The distinction is often a very delicate matter because, in therapy, ethical values must not be injured on either side if the treatment is to be successful. Yet what happens in the therapeutic process is only a special instance of human relationships in general. As soon as the dialogue between two people touches on something fundamental, essential, and numinous, and a certain rapport is felt, it gives rise to a phenomenon which Lévy-Bruhl fittingly called *participation mystique*. It is an unconscious identity in which two individual psychic spheres interpenetrate to such a degree that it is impossible to say what belongs to whom. If the problem is one of conscience, the guilt of the one partner is the guilt of the other, and at first there is no possibility of breaking this emotional identity. For this a special act of reflection is required. I have dwelt at some length on this problem because I wanted to show that by the concept of the archetype nothing final is meant, and that it would be wrong to suppose that the essence of conscience could be reduced to nothing but the archetype. The psychoid nature of the archetype contains very much more than can be included in a psychological explanation. It points to the sphere of the *unus mundus*,[5] the unitary world, toward which the psychologist and the atomic physicist are converging along separate paths, producing independently of each other certain analogous auxiliary concepts. Although the first step in the cognitive process is to discriminate and divide, at the second step it will unite what has been divided, and an explanation will be satisfactory only when it achieves a synthesis.

5. [Cf. *Mysterium Coniunctionis, Collected Works,* XIV (1963), Chapter VI, section 9.—TRANSLATOR.]

For this reason I have not been able to confine myself exclusively to the psychological nature of conscience, but have had to consider its theological aspect. From this point of view it cannot be presupposed that the act of conscience is something that, of its own nature, can be treated exhaustively by means of a rational psychology. We have, rather, to give priority to the assertion which conscience itself makes—that it is a voice of God. This view is not a contrivance of the intellect, it is a primary assertion of the phenomenon itself: a numinous imperative which from ancient times has been accorded a far higher authority than the human intellect. The daemon of Socrates was not the empirical person of Socrates. Conscience as such, if regarded objectively, without rationalistic assumptions, behaves like a God so far as its demands and authority are concerned, and asserts that it is God's voice. This assertion cannot be overlooked by an objective psychology, which must also include the irrational. Nor can it be pinned down to the question of truth, for this is unanswerable anyway and for epistemological reasons has long since become obsolete. Human knowledge has to be content with constructing models which are "probable"—it would be thoughtless presumption to demand more. For just as knowledge is not faith, so faith is not knowledge. We are concerned here with things that can be disputed, that is, with knowledge, but not with indisputable faith, which precludes critical discussion at the outset. The oft-repeated paradox "knowledge through faith" seeks in vain to bridge the gulf that separates the two.

When, therefore, the psychologist explains genuine conscience as a collision of consciousness with a numinous archetype, he may be right. But he will have to add at once that the archetype *per se,* its psychoid essence, cannot be comprehended, that it possesses a transcendence which it shares with the unknown substance of the psyche in general. The mythical assertion of conscience that it is the voice of God is an inalienable part of its nature, the foundation of its numen. It is as much a phenomenon as conscience itself.

In conclusion I would like to say that conscience is a psychic

reaction which one can call *moral* because it always appears
when the conscious mind leaves the path of custom, of the
mores, or suddenly recollects it. Hence in the great majority of
cases conscience signifies primarily the reaction to a real or
supposed deviation from the moral code, and is for the most
part identical with the primitive fear of anything unusual, not
customary, and hence "immoral." As this behavior is instinctive and, at best, only partly the result of reflection, it may be
"moral" but can raise no claim to being *ethical.* It deserves this
qualification only when it is reflective, when it is subjected to
conscious scrutiny. And this happens only when a fundamental
doubt arises as between two possible modes of moral behavior,
that is to say in a conflict of duty. A situation like this can be
"solved" only by suppressing one moral reaction, upon which
one has not reflected till now, in favor of another. In this case
the moral code will be invoked in vain, and the judging
intellect finds itself in the position of Buridan's ass between
two bundles of hay. Only the creative power of the ethos that
expresses the whole man can pronounce the final judgment.
Like all the creative faculties in man, his ethos flows empirically from two sources: from rational consciousness and from
the irrational unconscious. It is a special instance of what I
have called the transcendent function,[6] which is the discursive
cooperation of conscious and unconscious factors or, in theological language, of reason and grace.

It is not the task of psychological understanding to broaden
or to narrow the concept of conscience. "Conscience," in
ordinary usage, means the consciousness of a factor which in
the case of a "good conscience" affirms that a decision or an act
accords with morality and, if it does not, condemns it as
"immoral." This view, deriving as it does from the *mores,* from
what is customary, can properly be called "moral." Distinct
from this is the ethical form of conscience, which appears
when two decisions or ways of acting, both affirmed to be

---

6. [Cf. "The Transcendent Function," in *The Structure and Dynamics
of the Psyche, Collected Works,* VIII (1960), 67 ff.—Translator.]

moral and therefore regarded as "duties," collide with each other. In these cases, not foreseen by the moral code because they are mostly very individual, a judgment is required which cannot properly be called "moral" or in accord with custom. Here the decision has no custom at its disposal on which it could rely. The deciding factor appears to be something else: it proceeds not from the traditional moral code but from the unconscious foundation of the personality. The decision is drawn from dark and deep waters. It is true that these conflicts of duty are solved very often and very conveniently by a decision in accordance with custom, that is, by suppressing one of the opposites. But this is not always so. If one is sufficiently conscientious the conflict is endured to the end, and a creative solution emerges which is produced by the constellated archetype and possesses that compelling authority not unjustly characterized as the voice of God. The nature of the solution is in accord with the deepest foundations of the personality as well as with its wholeness; it embraces conscious and unconscious and therefore transcends the ego.

The concept and phenomenon of conscience thus contains, when seen in a psychological light, two different factors: on the one hand a recollection of, and admonition by, the *mores;* on the other, a conflict of duty and its solution through the creation of a third standpoint. The first is the moral, and the second the ethical, aspect of conscience.

INDEX